THE
WALKING
BOOK

ISBN 0-88176-322-5
Cover Design: Jeff Hapner

Table of Contents

Introduction

Are you convinced that exercise is not beneficial unless it hurts? Are you afraid to try vigorous activity because you have questions about your health? Do you believe that your twice-weekly tennis lessons are keeping you fit? Do you think that dieting is far better than exercising for weight loss because activity makes you hungry? Do you think you're too old or too young to begin a carefully planned walking program?

If you do, you've got another thing coming. We're about to give you all the information you need to begin and stay with an exercise program that can add years to your life and life to your years. It can help you lose weight faster than any diet alone. It can improve the efficiency of your heart and lungs, keep you flexible, heighten your awareness, and give you a new sense of confidence in your body.

In the following pages, you'll learn all about the undeniable benefits of walking, how easy it is to get started, what to look for in clothing and shoes, and how you can measure your success. You'll learn how walking can help you trim your body, relieve stress, and even slow down the aging process. People with special problems like obesity, arthritis, and emphysema will be delighted to learn that, yes, walking is for them, too.

Running—unlike walking—is not for everyone. It is physically demanding and even damaging if done improperly. A runner's knees and feet can suffer greatly. Although walkers may experience some physical discomfort (and this book will tell you how to deal with it), it is usually nothing like the aches, pains, and strains that regularly beset runners and joggers. Walking is invigorating and healthful, but not so demanding that you'll be exhausted.

About ten years ago, the national YMCA wanted to develop an exercise program that (1) did not require a lot of sophisticated testing; (2) permitted people to start exercising without having to see their doctor (unless they had a serious question about their health); (3) controlled their body weight; (4) improved their health quotient; (5) reduced selected coronary heart disease risk factors; and (6) improved their fitness level. The YMCA wanted a program that would keep people exercising, with few or no exercise dropouts. Walking became a central theme of the YMCA program. People who participated in early test classes made comments like, "I feel great," "I sleep better," "No more depression, no more high blood pressure," "I like myself better," "It's fun," "I love life more," and "I have more energy." Over 30 reasons were listed.

The men and women who participated improved their fitness levels and lowered their blood pressure and their cholesterol levels. Their depression and anxiety seemed to disappear. They felt good about themselves.

Surprisingly, no one mentioned losing weight—although that was the reason why the participants had signed up for the classes in the first place. But they did lose weight. Most of them shed about 10 pounds. However, the weight loss was no longer their only objective. What kept them going was their overall good feeling of well-being.

In 1978, at a three-day conference entitled "Exercise and Aging—Its Role in the Prevention of Physical Decline," held at the National Institute of Health at Bethesda, Maryland, researchers from the United States, Canada, and Western Europe presented papers stating that walking is the most efficient form of exercise, and the only one you can safely follow all the years of your life. We agree wholeheartedly.

It's our goal to make a believer of you, too.

The
Primitive Way

If you could go back in time and live the way the American pioneers did, would you? Would you trade places with the most isolated bands of Eskimos, whose life is—or used to be—one long, frigid struggle? Can you imagine yourself living as some of the more primitive tribes of Africa do—people whose way of life hasn't changed much since the Stone Age?

Probably not. But if we did go back to the primitive way, we'd be far more fit than we are now. Sophisticated as we members of technologically advanced societies are in our understanding of science and medicine, we can't consider ourselves superior to the primitives in fitness.

Thousands of years ago, walking was the best way or the only way to get around. Today, Australian aborigines still use their feet to secure the basic necessities of life. A group of them stalks a kangaroo mile after mile for days, until the kangaroo is too exhausted to go any further. Then they kill it for food and carry the carcass back the way they came—walking, mile after mile, until they arrive again at their home camp.

Surprisingly, once through the critical period of childhood infectious diseases, the aborigines live as long as the average American, without the help of medical technology.

There are a few other groups of people scattered through the mountain regions of Pakistan, Ecuador, and

Russia who have endurance like that of the aborigines. They use their bodies vigorously every day in everything they do. Theirs is a simpler life than we are used to, and it is much more physically active than ours. They eke out an existance that our culture views as primitive, but they live as long—if not longer—than those of us who live in "advanced" societies. These primitive peoples remain active, contributing, vigorous members of their societies right up to death.

Many of these isolated, primitive peoples have little resistance to microbial infections that merely inconvenience us. But they have a much greater resistance to heart disease, diabetes, and the more common forms of cancer—diseases that not only cut life short, but take away enjoyment of life.

Heart disease is the biggest killer of all diseases that plague advanced societies. However, researchers at the Australian National University found a tribe of natives in New Guinea in which heart disease is extremely rare and diabetes is unknown. Of 777 natives studied, only two had any sign of heart disease.

The investigation suggests what other studies on primitive societies have established: the resistance of primitive people to our ailments is not due primarily to genetic immunity, which would be able to protect them even after they began to lead modern lives. It seems certain that their relative freedom from degenerative disease is at least partly due to the fact that life in unmechanized surroundings requires human beings to function near their physical capacity in order to survive. There is growing evidence to support the theory that modern man's failure to use physical powers developed over thousands of years is responsible for his premature physical and mental degeneration.

If you want a specific example of how the sedentary ways of "civilization" offset so-called primitive societies, you have one fairly close to home. This process of physical debilitation has been dramatically documented by researchers studying Eskimos in the Canadian Arctic. In the old days, these hearty people lived a nomadic, self-reliant life. In numbing temperatures of 50 degrees below zero, the men hunted and fished; the women fished through the ice; and walking was always necessary. Now, however, the airplane links Eskimos everywhere with the 20th century. For all but a few of them, walking, driving dog sleds, and living in igloos are only memories. Today's Eskimos drive snowmobiles and live in electrified wooden houses built by the federal government. Once left to die in times of famine, infants and the elderly are now protected by welfare and pensions. But if the Eskimos are further from death than they used to be, they are also further from fitness. The men no longer have to hunt for food. Instead they work at sedentary factory jobs and take their meals in the company cafeteria, where they overeat. The women, who once tanned skins and made their family's clothes, can now purchase their clothing at stores. They have little to do but eat sweets and go to the movies. Bored with the tameness of settlement life, teenagers educated in Bureau of Indian Affairs schools nibble chocolate bars and drink soda pop.

As a result of this sheltered, inactive lifestyle, in one generation the Eskimos have begun to develop degenerative diseases at a frightening rate. Obesity, diabetes, heart disease, and other ailments are starting to weaken bodies that once thrived on the challenge of the frozen North.

It is revealing to compare the sedentary Eskimos with the long-lived people of Hunza in the Himalayas, Ecuador, and Abkhazia in Russia. These people walk everywhere possible. Just scrambling over the slopes of their mountainous homelands has given them a high degree of cardiovascular fitness. Tests showed that although these old people have many forms of heart and blood vessel disease, the oxygen supply to their hearts is so good that heart attacks do little harm.

Americans and members of other industrial societies had to work very hard 30, 40, or 50 years ago—so hard that fat was a luxury, a symbol of the leisure class. Most people lived in small towns or on farms, but even city dwellers did a fair amount of walking to work, to market, to visit friends, to parties, to dances. Strolling to and from an evening's entertainment was usually considered part of the entertainment. Getting there was half the fun. Two-story houses were the rule rather than the exception, so most people did a good deal of walking or running up and down stairs.

All this has changed. Modern devices have made us almost completely sedentary. For example, a small thing such as an extension phone in a home saves 70 miles of walking a year. For the average person this means a two-pound weight increase each year. Compare, too, the amount of human energy (calories) spent in using hand tools with the energy expended in using electric models today.

Back in the 1930s, the United States Research Council said that the average sedentary man needed 3,000 calories a day to maintain his body weight; the average woman needed around 2,400. Today, less than 50 years later, the council says a sedentary man requires approximately 2,400 calories a day to maintain that weight and the average female needs as little as 1,800.

Somewhere along the line we've cut 600 calories out of our lives: we burn 600 fewer calories every day. We're great at conserving our own physical energy, but for what purpose? All of this conservation has given us a new problem: obesity. Few people would be happy to go back to the days when everything had to be done by hand or by foot. But our grandparents didn't have to contend with obesity and its related problems.

The trends that encourage obesity are likely to continue. The more labor-saving devices we acquire—and it seems as though someone comes up with a new one every day—the fewer calories we burn away, and the more weight we gain. Inactivity is so much a part of our culture that we actually have to go out of our way to burn off calories. But unless we do, all the energy we're saving by sitting when we should be moving is converted into fat.

When we examine the daily activities of the hardy people who scramble after goats and walk up and down steep hills to gather food or just to bathe in a stream, it becomes clear that in most parts of the world technology has made this kind of vigorous living obsolete. Most of us do not have to walk or do much physical work, either in our occupations or at home. In our present way of life, physical performance is almost unnecessary. The result has been lower vitality. But our scientific sophistication makes us aware that disuse of the body's physical strength is contrary to our evolutionary heritage, and a new concept has emerged. This is *fitness:* the idea that the body's organs and muscles must be exercised regularly if an individual is to preserve a balance between physical and mental development and attain maximum well-being.

There is proof all around us that man should strive to condition his body to be able to bear the stresses of life. Each winter storm kills people who don't realize that shoveling snow can be lethal to the unfit. Sagging and expanding body contours are a constant reminder that lack of movement leads to muscular degeneration. Weakness, shortness of breath, aches and pains, tension and nervousness are common symptoms among today's white-collar workers. All can have their origin in insufficient physical activity. The human mind has achieved remarkable things, but it has yet to create an artificial substitute for exercise.

How can we regain our lost vitality? Do we have to hunt kangaroos or live in a mountain village and raise goats? No, but we must give our bodies 15 to 60 minutes of activity every day. The most vital point of an exercise program intended to maintain good physical condition is *consistency*, not duration or intensity. Walkers have to work, to be sure, but needn't exhaust themselves in order to reap startling benefits. And since walking is so convenient, participants should find it easy to be consistent.

Nostalgia is very big these days. Tiffany lamps, old Superman comic books, beer cans—anything that reminds us of the good old days is "in." Unfortunately, many Americans aren't nostalgic about the loss of their physical heritage. We need to be more primitive. We've got to get out there and walk.

The Advantages of Walking

For many years, many doctors have said that walking is excellent exercise. We think it's the perfect exercise because almost everyone can walk, without fancy paraphernalia, fees, or instructors. You can fit walking into your particular way of life more easily than almost any other kind of exercise.

Although not as strenuous as jogging, walking will increase your heart rate and oxygen consumption enough to qualify as an aerobic exercise. An aerobic exercise is the type that gets your whole body, or most of it, moving. It produces a "training effect" on your body by getting your heart to beat fast and your breath to become deep. This is the kind of effect marathon runners experience when they train. Aerobic exercise makes your body work better. Most doctors say true health begins with aerobic fitness.

Some people have found out, the hard way, that the use of crash diets and "wonder drugs" for losing weight can be futile or even dangerous. Instead they might have tried walking. Half an hour of vigorous striding burns 180 to 250 calories. A walk like this every day means a weight loss of 15 pounds in a year—without a change of eating habits. Physiologists calculate that 19 percent body fat is ideal for a woman and 15 percent is ideal for a man in terms of overall health. A lower ratio, down to as little as 5 percent fat, is safe and can be desirable for a svelte appearance. Walking can help you maintain a low percentage of body fat.

Walking helps other parts of your body, too. Your digestive system can be made healthier through walking: it stimulates elimination and helps reduce constipation. Walking improves circulation in your legs, which means you can avoid getting varicose veins. Better circulation to your leg muscles can mean less leg fatigue and fewer aches. Walking improves muscle tone in the legs, making them more shapely and healthy-looking. Walking is a natural tranquilizer: it can reduce anxiety and tension. Even depression can be relieved. And walking can lower dynamic blood pressure; that is, your blood pressure under stress.

There are plenty of exercises for which similar claims can be made. However, there is one fact that makes walking best of all for many people: the only exercise that does you any good is the exercise you do; and walking is very easy. It is less demanding that other aerobic exercises like swimming and running. If you're in reasonably good health—free of chest pain, dizziness, and high blood pressure—and if you use good judgment, you shouldn't have any problems. Except in rare cases, you shouldn't need medical clearance, and you certainly won't need the kind of extensive physical exam that is recommended for more strenuous exercise programs. (For safety's sake you should tell your doctor that you're interested in beginning a walking program, but if you use some common sense, you shouldn't have trouble.)

Even heart disease sufferers, the overweight, and people with arthritis and emphysema can enjoy the benefits of walking. At the very least, your senses and your awareness of the world around you will be enhanced and heightened. Things will look better to you, and one day you will realize that your psychological well-being matches the improvement in your body.

AEROBIC CAPACITY: A TEST FOR FITNESS

Experts measure a person's fitness in terms of aerobic capacity; that is, the ability to pick up oxygen, send it throughout the body, and use it. This capacity can be measured by an exercise stress test. During such a test, you pedal a stationary bicycle, walk or run on a motorized treadmill, or step on and off a bench—under a doctor's close supervision. Your electrocardiogram is continuously monitored, and your blood pressure is observed to guard against overexertion. At the first sign that the heart is irritated by exercise, the test is stopped. By watching the electrocardiogram, your blood pressure, and your respiration rate, the doctor can tell when you are working to your capacity. The test also involves a measurement of oxygen use. During this part of the test, you breathe into a one-way valve that lets the doctor collect the exhaled air. The air is then analyzed to determine how much oxygen your body used during the activity. The amount of oxygen used represents your aerobic capacity.

Most people do poorly in these tests. It's no wonder, then, that adults completely run out of steam by four or five o'clock in the afternoon. They lack the energy they once had. This is a sign of poor aerobic capacity. Your lungs, heart, blood vessels, and muscles are kept at peak efficiency if you challenge them frequently with regular activity; if you do not, they will start to atrophy or weaken. Their ability to function will be reduced, and you will lose stamina.

Aerobic capacity can be improved by proper walking. When you walk, your heart starts to beat faster and move large amounts of oxygen-rich blood around your body more forcefully. Your blood vessels expand to carry this oxygen. In your working muscles, dormant (unused) blood vessels open up to permit a good pick-up of oxygen and release of carbon dioxide. These changes improve your ability to process oxygen.

Your heart rates during activity and at rest will be reduced greatly. That means your heart will pump more blood with each beat. It's like tuning your car to get more miles to the gallon. The heart of an average adult at rest beats 60 to 80 times a minute. A well-trained heart at rest may beat 40 to 50 times, or even less, a minute. Many people begin an exercise program with a resting heart rate of 80 beats a minute. After three months of walking, it drops to 60; a year later it might stabilize at 50. At that lowest rate, the heart is beating 35,000 fewer times a day than it did before the program began.

At the beginning of a walking program, a person's pulse rate may reach 130 or 140 beats a minute after 20 to 30 minutes of walking. But as weeks go by, the heart becomes more efficient, and the exercise heart rate is lower during the 20 to 30 minutes of walking. To continue enjoying the training effect of walking, the walker must walk faster, or occasionally longer.

A recent study set out to explore the importance of different kinds of exercise. The researchers wanted to find out how walking compared with other forms of exercise, such as jogging, gymnastics, and various athletic games. To do this, the researchers chose 16 healthy but sedentary men between the ages of 40 and 56. These men walked from two and a half to three and a half miles each day, four days a week for 20 weeks. As they walked, they tried to keep their heart beat rates within a certain training range. To test the effectiveness of the walking program, the 16 men were tested on a treadmill. While on the treadmill, their oxygen-intake capacities were measured. Their heart rate responses to a standard treadmill walk and to a one-mile walk were also measured. The results: a fast walk can be as effective as a slow jog. The men were able to walk longer at a lower heart beat rate by the end of the 20 weeks. Their oxygen-intake capacity improved. In fact, the researchers said, "The training heart rate data show walking to be a moderate to rigorous activity which has sufficient intensity to cause a significant training effect."

The study's group of walkers had to move faster and faster to keep their heart beat rates in the proper range. After the 20 weeks of training, when the men walked at a certain speed on the treadmill, their heart rates were about 17 beats slower than what they were at the beginning of the training program. These results have been supported by many other studies.

How quickly your heart recovers after exercise is

a strong indicator of how fit you are. In the test group, the recovery rates dropped very fast. Recovery heart rates at one, three, and five minutes after exercise were about 19 to 24 beats per minute slower than when the program began. In other words, the 16 test subjects experienced the training effect, which shows that walking is excellent for building stamina and endurance. That's why walking helps you overcome late afternoon fatigue.

You can start a walking program as you would another type of exercise regimen, setting aside a specific time of day, buying yourself a special walking outfit, joining or forming a walking club. Or you can work it into your present life style so gradually that walking will not noticeably interfere with anything else you do.

A New York cardiologist tells his patients to get off the subway two exits early and walk the rest of the way. The doctor follows his own prescription, for he often walks down 15 flights of stairs from high in a New York hospital instead of riding the elevator.

One corporate executive has found a way to make good use of layover time between airplanes. If she has a two-hour wait between flights, she rents a locker in the airport terminal. She takes off her street shoes and puts on her hiking shoes. Then she puts the rest of her belongings in the locker and takes off for a walk around the terminal. She sees all sorts of interesting sights and enjoys herself immensely—more than most people do during a layover or a flight delay. And all the while she is improving her good health and trim figure.

WALKING IS FOR MEN AND WOMEN

We hope you agree with the statement above, and we hope you're wondering why we felt we had to say so. Unfortunately, some women avoid rigorous physical exercise because of a socialized bias against it, and some men believe walking is not strenuous enough to have a significant effect on fitness. The truth is walking can be beneficial to men and women, because the fitness needs of the two sexes are nearly identical.

Research has shown that—except for upper body strength, lean body weight, and height—there is little difference in the overall strength, endurance and body composition of male and female athletes. And, although the female may weigh less than the male, the ratio of fat to overall weight of physically fit men and women is just about the same. Because of these similarities, and because their needs are essentially the same, there is little reason to advocate different training or conditioning programs on the basis of sex.

Women have different fitness needs only in the sense that they need exercise even more than men: the average woman is less fit than the average man. The reason is cultural, not biological. American cultural patterns—and even some exercise experts—tend to overprotect women and discourage them from physical activity after puberty. Over the years, popular culture has prized a shapely female figure; yet it has also perpetuated the myth that exercise is unfeminine. The fact is that exercise is a necessity for women who want to develop and maintain attractive bodies.

Times are changing, and that's good. Research has clearly demonstrated the value of exercise in good health and beauty, so increasing numbers of young women are exercising. But cultural biases against vigorous exercise still exist, especially among women past 35. Many of these women like walking because it is "safe" and socially non-threatening. There probably are four reasons why walking is a great way for women to ease into exercise: they don't have to be proficient at athletics: they can combine walking with other activities and therefore work a walking program into a busy schedule; no special clothing is needed; and walking is a low-sweat exercise.

Take a look at any of the leading women's magazines. Chances are, you'll see photographs of women running, bicycling, or playing tennis; but they never seem to work up a sweat. Some women remain convinced that exercise will ruin their hair, soak their clothes, run their mascara and enlarge their calves to unattractive proportions. Even if this were true, the effects of a lack of exercise are far worse.

Many women who today do not like to exercise feel the way they do because they were excused from physical education in high school for a lot of silly reasons. Overprotective parents and doctors, and misinformed physical education teachers deprived girls and young women of the early training that would have inspired them to keep fit.

Walking can change all of this. Once women start walking, they begin to feel better mentally and physically, so they develop an interest in doing other physical things. Many women have become avid runners, tennis players, golfers, and squash and racquetball players after taking up walking. The walking helped them become physical beings. And suddenly many of them discover that migraine headaches, menstrual discomforts, depression and other problems disappear. The walking also improves their appearance, so their self-concept improves. Now they feel good about themselves, and see clearly that exercising is the right thing to do. Walking has liberated them from restrictive attitudes. They are now ready for increased activity. If they'd tried swimming or tennis as an initial activity, some of these women would have quit after a few sessions. But walking succeeded in pulling them into a more active life style. Today's modern woman understands that motion is important in her life. If she wants to live her life to the fullest, she needs to exercise.

Men have a problem with sweat, too. Only this time it is the reverse. Many men think the only good exercise is exercise that hurts and makes them sweat like a horse. Consequently, some men play basketball once a week in rubberized sweatsuits. They certainly do sweat a lot, and they think that will keep them fit. In fact, however, they're headed for heart, muscle, and joint trouble.

Some men run for fitness. That's fine. But what isn't fine are judgmental statements such as, "girls walk; running is for men." That attitude stems from a man's younger days. When in school, many boys run to get into shape. They run wind sprints at the end of the sports practice and more laps when disciplined. Unlike women, men are expected to run in their teenage years.

This is good training for performance. It makes sense. But we're concerned with fitness, not sports. Fitness means improved heart-lung function that will help you get through the day without excessive fatigue. Fitness means control of your body weight. It also implies reducing the risk of coronary heart disease and making you feel better. In other words, the goal of fitness is to help you achieve better health and well-being. Unfortunately, many men think fitness and sports are synonymous.

For all these reasons, men think running is far better than walking to get into shape. So they run. But soon many of them grow to dislike it. They remember the wind sprints, the laps, and all the other distasteful things about high school sports and never get around to exercising on a permanent basis. They know they need exercise. They talk about it, but they don't want to get involved and be committed to it. Instead, they play their basketball once a week and expect that to do the job. It won't.

Even worse are instances of out-of-shape men who insist upon engaging in physical activities that are beyond their capabilities. Running sometimes encourages this, with overweight or unprepared men pushing their bodies beyond safe limits in order to pick up their pace or finish a marathon. These unhappy fellows have not realized that the most important ingredient in fitness is how consistently, not how hard, you work. Running is a super way to get fit. So are bicycling and swimming—if you do them regularly and approach them in a sane manner. But many men don't. The best way to start a fitness program is by walking. Take your time and see what happens.

Many men ease into a new program of walking fitness by incorporating it into their daily routine—by making a point to stride up and down the halls at work, or by walking to the restaurant at lunchtime instead of driving. The opportunities for good health and enjoyment are there—no man should give up the joy of walking.

Nor should women. Nor should people of either sex who have specific physical problems. They shouldn't allow themselves to believe that they can't benefit from walking. Walking is for everybody.

Your Healthy Heart

Medical casebooks are full of heart cases deemed "hopeless." Doctors shake their heads, spouses cry, and patients go along with the diagnosis and quietly die. But sometimes a heart patient will defy the odds, decide that he or she is going to live, and embark upon a sensible program of exercise. For such patients, walking is the ideal way to regain strength, health, and life itself.

It should be emphasized that no single program of walking—or exercise of any sort—is ideal for *all* recovering heart patients. But those patients who are realistic and willing to listen to their bodies as well as to their doctors will probably be rewarded.

ADDING YEARS TO YOUR LIFE

Many people refuse to believe that exercise will lead to a longer life. They point to statistics that seem to show that, although Americans are becoming increasingly sedentary, they are living longer.

However, when the United States is compared with all of the world's other countries in terms of longevity, the U.S. doesn't measure up: the American male ranks 22nd and the American female ranks 10th. Recent statistics show that the U.S. ranks 37th in life expectancy for men 40 years of age. Twenty years ago, we were 11th. Today, an American boy or girl may have a life expectancy of around 66 and 71 years of age. That appears to be a significant improvement over the life expectancy as calculated in 1900: around 47 to 49 years. But these figures are deceptive. The life expectancy figures do not give the actual age when most people die. Instead, the figures simply tell you the average age of death when you lump all the ages together. In those countries that have a high infant death rate, the average life expectancy is quite low. It is low even though many people live to an advanced age. But when medicine can save the lives of small children, life expectancy figures for the entire population soar.

This is why our life expectancy appears to have risen over the years. Until the 1850s, only half the children born in the U.S. reached the age of five. Today, almost 98 percent make it to that age. That fact is bound to pull up our life expectancy. In 1790, a 60-year-old veteran of the American Revolution had a life expectancy of about 15 more years. Incredibly, his 60-year-old counterpart today has almost the same number of years to live. So it appears that even though we are increasing our longevity as a nation, individuals in America are not living longer than they did 100 or 200 years ago.

The reason why we are not living longer is that degenerative diseases (particularly heart disease) are cutting our lives short. What is especially depressing is that these degenerative diseases also rob us of the "good life." We're tired before the end of the day. Walking is an effort. Life has no joy. Things are too much of a hassle. Our productivity is curtailed. Many of us are not running on all or our cylinders because we suffer from one or more of these modern plagues.

We think exercise can reverse this process. Some critics may say that there is not enough evidence to prove that all people who exercise live longer than people who don't. That is so. But on the other hand, research has not been able to prove the contrary. And while there are many variables regarding exercise and longevity, research is starting to move closer to definite conclusions.

A study of 500 men who died in Boston in 1965 asked close relatives questions about smoking, eating, exercise, sleeping, recreation, and occupational habits— more than 200 factors. The researchers then arranged the data, looking for interactions of these factors relative to longevity. The results were fascinating: (1) physical exertion during leisure hours benefited people more than exertion on the job; and (2) physical exertion off the job, particularly during the years 40 to 49, were among the best of all longevity predictors. It has been estimated that coronary heart disease robs the average American of seven to 11 years of life. In other words, if coronary heart disease were eliminated, the average American would live seven to 11 years longer than he or she does now.

A large-scale health survey based on a study of 7,000 adults in California over a long period of time demonstrated an 11.5-year greater life expectancy for people whose life styles incorporated six or seven basic health requirements versus those with three or fewer of them. You've probably already guessed the factors. They were: (1) moderate, regular exercise; (2) normal weight; (3) breakfast every day; (4) regular meals with no snacks in between; (5) seven or eight hours of sleep per night; (6) moderate drinking (one small drink or less daily); and (7) no smoking. The findings of this California study were duplicated in a Wisconsin study on 2,000 people.

A few of you may protest. You might say, "I know a guy who exercised regularly every day of his life and he died of a heart attack at 46." But this is a function of heredity. No one can guarantee that if you "live right" you will live longer than your sedentary brethren. If you exercise, you'll get closer to your potential for old age; yet you may not live longer than your sedentary neighbor. Sound contradictory? It isn't. Here's why.

The latest research seems to indicate that we inherit our parents' potential for longevity and fitness. Then our circumstances and the choices we make each day chop months or years away from that allotted life span and influence the degree of our fitness and longevity. For example, although genetically, your parents may have had the capacity to live to be 100, perhaps their circumstances and their habits caused them to die much earlier than that. Likewise, although you may have inherited the capacity to live to be 100, your environment and your habits—many of which are learned from your parents—may enable you to live only to the age of 65 or 70. What's more, if you live in noisy, polluted surroundings and do "head work" all day long, forgetting to exercise your senses, your muscles, and your organs, you will forfeit your potential for fitness and longevity.

THE SPECTER OF HEART DISEASE

Coronary artery disease is responsible for the deaths of almost 700,000 people in this country every year. It has been estimated that 12 million Americans are currently being treated for heart disease; another 12 million have it and don't know it. This high rate of coronary disease is largely responsible for the relatively poor life expectancy rate of males in the United States.

If over 10 percent of the population were to come down with some kind of exotic virus or flu, there would be great public uproar. Yet we accept coronary heart disease as an inevitable occurrence, just one of those things: pimples at 13, a coronary at 50. This is a real tragedy, for some cardiologists feel that heart disease can be prevented or postponed so that it won't occur before the age of 70.

Heart disease is a complicated ailment. Many factors are involved, including body weight, diet, activity, blood fats, and others. It is important to remember that walking is just one limited part of treating this disease. Fitness, like medicine, is not a magic cure-all in its effects on the human circulatory system.

The circulatory system includes the heart, arteries, veins, and capillaries. This system circulates blood to all parts of your body. The blood provides body tissues with oxygen and food, and removes waste.

The heart is made of muscle tissue called the myocardium. Like all muscles, the heart must have a continuous blood supply. But blood doesn't simply rush through the heart. It is sent through a special set of arteries, the coronary arteries, which surround the myocardium.

Human beings have a unique need for a "second heart." Four-legged animals don't need such a second heart because all their vital organs are on the same level. The heart, brain, lungs, and even the reproductive glands of four-legged creatures have an easy time getting all the blood they need. But human beings stand upright, so the human circulatory system has to cope with gravity. Nature had to devise a way to pump the blood straight up. The muscles around the veins are pressed into service. Muscles in your feet, calves, thighs, buttocks, and abdomen compose this second heart. As they work, they rhythmically contract and release, squeezing the veins and forcing the blood along, easing the load of pushing 72,000 quarts of blood through your system every 24 hours through nearly 100,000 miles of circulatory byways. It's nature's way of moving the blood to the heart despite the pull of gravity. These second heart muscles work best when you walk.

The key to the efficiency of the circulatory system is walking. Walking makes the muscles below the waist do their part in helping the heart. Without this help, there can be unhappy consequences sometimes, like varicosities or phlebitis. The heart must work harder when it doesn't get assistance from your leg muscles.

For this reason, (and many others) walking has become important in the treatment of heart patients. Doctors now know that walking is the best way to make the lower muscles do their share of the work and relieve a damaged heart. Even a little walking improves circulation and costs the heart no effort. Surprisingly, people whose heart rate and blood pressure are high will find that daily walking helps bring the heart rate and blood pressure down to more normal levels.

A heart attack is not primarily a disease of the heart muscle, but of the arteries that supply the heart muscle with blood. The heart, just like any other muscle, receives its blood supply from the arteries that run through it.

In the anatomy of the human heart, an extensive network of arteries grows out from two main trunks, the right and left coronary arteries. These branch out much like a tree. Each branch is smaller than the main trunk, and each one subdivides into smaller branches. Those in turn divide into still smaller ones, like tiny twigs. Every part of the heart, no matter how small, is supplied with blood and oxygen through the system of coronary arteries, vessels, and capillaries.

In order to understand coronary heart disease, it is important to become familiar with the following terms.

Arteriosclerosis: A general term for various types of arterial illness. The phrase, "hardening of the arteries" is often used for arteriosclerosis. It is associated with a gradually increasing brittleness of arteries.

Atherosclerosis: Slowly developing disease of the coronary arteries. In atherosclerosis, the passageway through the arteries becomes roughened and narrowed by fatty deposits that harden into patches along the inner lining of the artery. Consequently, the channel is gradually narrowed, and there is less room for blood to flow through.

Coronary occlusion: A severe narrowing of some coronary artery to the point that blood can no longer pass through.

Coronary thrombosis: A coronary occlusion caused by the formation of a blood clot (thrombus) that completely blocks the flow of blood to some part of the heart muscle.

Myocardial infarction: A condition in which the blood supply to a portion of the muscle is blocked, causing the muscle fed by the blocked artery to die.

Loafer's Heart: A term describing the weakening of the heart muscle as a result of a lack of exercise. It is not the so-called athlete's heart, which should not be considered abnormal for that is a strong and well-developed heart, but the degenerated, inadequate loafer's heart that is a cause for concern.

Collateral circulation: The opening of new arteries and the growth of new branches to offset the effects of atherosclerosis. It is fortunate that the coronary system is able to grow and repair itself. When some of the coronary arteries become narrowed by gradual development of atherosclerosis, nearby arteries get wider and even open up tiny new branches to bring blood to the area of the heart that needs it. Collateral circulation explains why many people who have a narrow artery do not suffer heart attacks and also accounts for some of the excellent recoveries from attacks.

BENEFITS OF EXERCISE

Hundreds of studies have been conducted worldwide to determine why so many people develop heart disease. The causes remain very much a mystery, although many researchers believe they've found a relationship between exercise and healthy hearts. It seems that people who are very active are less likely to suffer heart disease than people who seldom exercise.

A study of two groups of adults in Switzerland showed the relationship between heart disease and lack of exercise. One group was from a mountain village called Blattendorf. These people were compared with a similar group of adults who lived in the town of Basel. The residents of Blattendorf lived several miles from the nearest cart path. So the mountain villagers had to walk everywhere. Climbing mountains and carrying heavy loads were part of their daily routine. They had a much lower percentage of heart disease than did the sedentary inhabitants of Basel, who did very little walking. Studies from all over the world have supported the findings of the Swiss study. In the early 1950s, the health records of 31,000 double-decker bus workers in London were studied. The active conductors who frequently walked around the bus and climbed the stairs were found to have a lower mortality rate and a remarkably faster recovery rate from heart attacks than did the inactive bus drivers.

In 1973, a group of doctors did a different kind of study. Instead of comparing the incidence of heart disease among people in physically active and inactive occupations, the researchers studied the amount of leisure-time exercise in which the people were involved. All aspects of their life style, except for the amount of exercise they got, were the same. The report of the study speaks for itself: "Eleven percent of the men who developed coronary disease, compared with twenty-six percent of the controls, reported vigorous activity. In men recording vigorous exercise the relative risk of developing coronary disease was about a third of that in comparable men who did not, and in men reporting much of it still less. Vigorous exercise apparently protected against rapid fatal heart attacks and other first clinical attacks of coronary disease alike, throughout middle age."

Exactly how strong is the relationship between heart disease and inactivity? In 1977, a ten-year study that focused on 17,000 Harvard alumni men aged 35 to 74 was reported upon. A specific finding was that those men who burned up less than 2,000 calories a week in exercise were 64 percent more likely to suffer a heart attack than those who burned more than that. Of the 572 heart attacks suffered by the group, the study estimated that 166 would never have happened if the men had exercised vigorously. And the study added that it didn't really matter what kind of exercise was performed, provided the exercise placed a demand on the heart. Golf, bowling, and archery did not qualify, but walking, jogging, swimming, and other demanding activities did.

A recent meeting of scientists in New York City addressed itself to marathon running. At that meeting, the experts concluded that people who adopted the life style of a marathon runner (who is able to run 26.2 miles nonstop, train 36-plus miles a week, and does not smoke) had very little likelihood of developing a coronary. One physician went so far as to say that this type of life style provides *immunity* from coronary artery disease. Many doctors, including the scientists at that New York meeting, would shy away from that assertion. But one thing is clear: a marathoner's way of life would greatly reduce your chances of having a heart attack.

WHY DOES WALKING WORK?

Walking can reduce *many* of your risk factors—those things that increase your chances of having a heart attack—not just one. There are 11 factors that affect your chances of getting coronary heart disease: heredity, stress, diet, fat abnormalities, hypertension, heart beat abnormalities, diabetes, obesity, smoking, age, and lack of physical activity. Of these 11, walking may improve all except age and heredity. Of course, smoking and diet are not altered by walking itself. Usually, however, people who walk on a regular basis adopt more healthful life styles. They often stop smoking, or cut back substantially, and start eating less. They also tend to eat wholesome foods, because they become more in tune with their bodies.

A recent study demonstrated the connection between a person's level of aerobic capacity and selected coronary heart disease risk factors. The conclusion was unavoidable: as a person's fitness level improved, his coronary heart disease risk factors drop substantially. The heart disease risk factors affected were cholesterol, triglycerides, glucose, uric acid, systolic blood pressure, and body fat measurements. Men of very poor or poor aerobic fitness showed poor results; those of fair aerobic fitness appeared to be less prone to heart ailments than those in the very poor or poor categories. But they were not as good as those in the excellent category. Those people who scored good and excellent on the aerobic fitness test had the lowest scores on the selected heart disease risk factors. The study involved 2,998 men with an average age of 44.6 years. It didn't matter which aerobic activity was used for fitness as long as the men got enough exercise to move into the good or excellent fitness category.

Although it is clear that walking helps the heart, blood, and blood vessels, no one knows exactly why. Aerobic exercise (including walking) may:

1. Increase the number and size of your blood vessels for better and more efficient circulation.

2. Increase the elasticity of the blood vessels and thereby reduce the likelihood of their breaking under pressure.

3. Increase the efficiency of exercising muscles and blood circulation so that muscles and blood are better able to pick up, carry, and use oxygen.

4. Increase the efficiency of the heart, making it able to pump more blood with fewer beats and better able to handle emergencies.

5. Increase tolerance to stress and give you more joy of living, which means you will be less likely to be caught in the stress/pressure syndrome.

6. Decrease triglyceride (fats) and cholesterol levels so as to reduce the likelihood of fats being deposited on the lining of the arteries.

7. Decrease clot formation so there is a smaller chance of a blood clot forming and blocking blood flow to the heart muscle.

8. Decrease blood sugar, reducing chances of blood sugar being changed into triglycerides.

9. Decrease obesity and high blood pressure, which is good since most people who are obese and have high blood pressure are more prone to heart disease.

10. Decrease hormone production—good because too much adrenalin can cause problems for the arteries.

Of all the above reasons, the most controversial has been No. 6; that is, that exercise will decrease triglyceride and cholesterol levels. Perhaps no other area has been subject to more controversy.

Doctors now know that it's not the quantity of cholesterol that's important, but how the cholesterol is carried. In your bloodstream, cholesterol is contained within several different types of large conglomerates of proteins and fatty substances. Surprisingly, cholesterol only misbehaves when it falls in with the wrong crowd.

A cholesterol molecule that is bound up with a high-density lipoprotein (HDL) is probably on its way back to the liver to be excreted back into the intestinal tract and eliminated from the body. Cholesterol carried by a low-density lipoprotein (LDL), on the other hand, is meant to be taken up by the body cells as a building block for hormones and cell membranes. Although this lipoprotein is necessary, when there is too much of it in the blood it is not good. Some of it will probably help build up atherosclerotic plaques on the insides of arteries.

Scientists theorize that HDL cholesterol can actually interfere with the process of atherosclerosis. The HDLs may pick up the extra cholesterol in the body and take it back to the liver for removal from the body. A high amount of HDL and a low level of LDL seems to offer some insurance against atherosclerosis. People with low levels of HDL cholesterol have eight times the rate of heart disease as those with higher levels. Fewer LDLs means there is less likelihood of the cholesterol being deposited on the lining of the arteries; more HDLs means more cholesterol is carried for removal from the body.

It now appears that regular, vigorous exercise is helpful in providing a desirable HDL-LDL ratio. Studies show that people who participate in an aerobic-type exercise program for 30 to 45 minutes four times a week find that their HDL levels begin to climb after only seven to 10 weeks.

Another controversial area is the effect of exercise on high blood pressure. Although many doctors now use walking as an adjunct to hypertension therapy, disagreement is everywhere.

One area in which there is little disagreement is the effect of walking on your dynamic blood pressure. Your dynamic blood pressure is a measure of your blood pressure throughout the day, not just the reading you get at the doctor's office. Your blood pressure can drop or climb throughout the day. During relaxing moments it is probably low; when you're feeling stress, it may zoom upward. Many doctors now feel that the real benefit of exercise is that it helps modulate your dynamic blood pressure. You'll still have valleys and peaks, for you're still subjected to pressures throughout the day. But exercise, such as walking, will see to it that the peaks are not as high as they used to be.

How much exercise do you need to enjoy the 10 positive changes mentioned as by-products of aerobic exercise? How much exercise do you need to have a good HDL-LDL ratio? And how much exercise do you need to keep your dynamic blood pressure from fluctuating too much?

Doctors are still trying to successfully answer these complex questions. But 45 minutes or more of walking at your target heart rate, four times a week, seems to do it for most people. Yet walking is not a panacea for heart disease. You may have to make other modifications in your living pattern to reduce your risk factors. Select foods carefully; deal with stress in a positive manner; don't smoke.

Recent statistics released by the National Institute of Health show that the incidence of fatal heart disease has decreased by about 14 percent among Americans over the past 20 years. Three reasons given for this drop are better dietary habits, less smoking, and more exercise. Significantly, the most important change was that exercise habits improved.

Walking is a positive approach to better quality of life and health. Walking is something you can actually look forward to; not something to avoid. You don't go to movies you dislike, you don't read books that are boring, you select your friends with care. So why pick an exercise program you won't like?

Losing Weight

It's not difficult to find so-called weight control experts who doubt the effectiveness of exercise as a method of weight reduction. They hold two misconceptions. First, they say exercise demands relatively little caloric expenditure and is therefore inefficient; and second, they believe exercise increases the appetite and is self-defeating as a weight control method.

Let's look at the first misconception. The body maintains a fine balance between the number of calories taken in and the number of calories burned up through physical activity. For example, if a person takes in 2,400 calories in a day and burns up 2,400 calories during sleeping, eating, working, walking, etc., he will maintain his present body weight. But if he eats 2,400 calories in a day and burns up only 2,300, he will have 100 calories left over. Those excess calories will then be stored as fat in the fat cells in the body until they are needed.

Physiologists tell us that approximately 3,500 calories equal one pound of fat. It doesn't matter what type of food is eaten—nutritious food or "junk"—it all contains calories, and they all count. So if 100 calories remain unburned at the end of each day for 35 days, the body will gain one pound of fat. By the end of a year, the body will have gained 10 pounds at that rate. This is the cumulative nature of weight gain.

This sort of slow gain that most people experience has been called "creeping obesity." Usually, weight gain is noticed over a period of months or years, not overnight.

One year you buy a 36-inch belt; the next year you need a 38-inch one.

Walking can be used to turn this process around—sort of a beneficial "creeping fat loss." At your brisk walking speed, you may have to walk for 12 hours to burn up one pound of fat, but it need not be done in a single 12-hour period. Half an hour of walking every day can result in a 15-pound weight loss each year. Extend each walk to an hour, and you can expect to lost 30 pounds. Many times, a 30-minute walk each day is all you need to get yourself back into caloric balance and then start losing weight.

Does this seem to be an exaggeration? Again, we'll let the facts speak for themselves. Time and motion studies have shown that the average overweight person walks about 2.2 miles a day; a person of average build walks 4.8 miles a day. The difference of 2.6 miles is the caloric equivalent of 200 to 300 calories a day—20 to 30 pounds a year.

Now for the second misconception: the belief that an increase in physical activity is a self-defeating weight control method because it increases appetite. Exercise does indeed increase the appetite of normally active people. This is one of the body's protective mechanisms. Without it, the body of a person who walks an hour extra each day, thereby expending the caloric equivalent of 30 pounds a year, obviously would burn away to nothing over a period of four or five years. The increase in hunger makes it possible to exercise without undermining well-being.

However, the principle does not work in reverse. If you decrease your activity below a moderate level, you will not decrease your appetite. In fact, your appetite will probably increase with inactivity. For many people, eating is a nervous habit. It's something they do just to keep their hands busy. When they're watching TV, sitting is not enough. They seem to like to have a beverage in one hand and potato chips or pretzels in another. Or if they go to a coffee klatch, it's a natural thing to be balancing a sweet roll and a cup of coffee (laced with sugar and cream) on their laps. When you are just sitting around doing next to nothing, you tend to eat more.

Observations of laboratory animals and human beings support this. A Harvard study of the relationship between food intake, exercise, and weight in white mice showed that the sedentary mice ate more than the moderately active group and slowly gained weight. The mice that exercised most ate more than the moderately active group, but they had the lowest weight of all the mice. The moderately active mice ate less than the other two groups. Their weight was right in the middle, halfway between the sedentary mice and the very active mice. Another study—this one of overweight high-school girls—showed that the same thing is true for human beings. The overweight girls ate no more and some ate less than their normal-weight classmates. However, the overweight girls exercised far less and went in for "sitting" activities. They spent four times as many hours watching TV as the others. Similar studies on boys revealed the same pattern.

A growing number of physicians who specialize in obesity agree with these findings. They believe that obesity is a physical activity problem; not a nutrition problem. Several years ago, *Lancet*, the highly respected British medical journal, summed it up in one brief sentence: "In obesity, sloth may be more important than gluttony."

DIETING ISN'T ENOUGH

That sentence seems to imply that putting an end to gluttony does not produce the desired lean, healthy look. This has been the observation of people who have lost weight. They often complain that they still look flabby. The reason is that when most people diet to lose weight, they lose both fat and lean body tissue. Lean body tissue is the bone-muscle-organ tissue of your body. Lean body tissue gives you your shape, and you don't want to lose it. A loss of lean tissue causes a saggy appearance. Exercise is better than dieting, then, because activity burns up fat but will not cause you to lose lean body tissue.

A study conducted at Kent State University illustrates this point nicely. The study set out to compare the effects of several different methods of weight reduction on the body. The 25 women who participated in the study were all between the ages of 25 and 40 and were 20 to 40 pounds overweight. Three groups were formed: (1) eight women who dieted only, reducing their caloric intake by 500 calories a day but holding their physical activity constant; (2) nine who continued to eat as usual, but increased their physical activity to burn off 500 extra calories a day; and (3) eight who reduced their caloric intake by 250 calories a day and increased physical activity to burn off another 250 calories. Before and after the 16-week period, the subjects were tested for body weight, body density, skin fold and girth measurements, and selected blood fats.

By the end of the study, women in all three groups had lost about the same amount of weight. The average individual weight loss in each group was 11.4 pounds, proof that all methods were extremely effective in controlling weight. However, the significant finding of the study was that there was a difference in body composition.

Those in the diet-only group lost some fat, but they also lost some lean body tissue; those in the combination diet-exercise group lost more fat than the dieters, and actually gained some lean tissue; the exercise group lost about the same amount of fat as the combination group, but they gained the greatest amount of lean tissue. The women in the exercise group were judged to look best by the end of the program.

The members of the exercise group also had more stamina than the others; their circulatory systems were much better able to withstand the rigors of exercise. The report concluded that the use of exercise in a weight reduction program is far superior to dieting alone in its effect on body composition and physical fitness.

Walking also helps people get out of the guilt trap of dieting. People who exercise regularly realize that they can "cheat" a little on special occasions without feeling guilty. They know that if they eat too much, they can simply walk a little extra distance to burn up those extra calories. They have the right idea. They have learned how to pay the price for living in modern-day America. And they like the way they look.

Relieving Stress

Henry Thoreau did it. Harry Truman, Abe Lincoln, and Albert Einstein did it. Robert Louis Stevenson, Adlai Stevenson, Conrad Adenauer, and Paul Dudley White were all members of the walking fraternity. Many famous people extolled the virtues of walking. Their day was incomplete without their "daily constitutional."

They weren't successful because they walked, but walking certainly helped them become more complete beings. They got more out of life. Walking helped relax and recharge their minds and bodies.

Recently, scientists have tried to explain why walking exercises your mind. Many feel that a period of brisk walking each day is essential for good health, including mental well-being.

Unfortunately, many people are unaware of the relationship between walking and the mind. To these people, the mind and the body are seperate entities. Yet your physical condition affects your psychological well-being and vice versa. This isn't a new idea. The average urban person is underactive but overstimulated. Actual physical danger is rare, but stress and anxiety are prevalent. You are not challenged by saber-toothed tigers or invading barbarians the way your ancestors were. Instead, your boss yells at you, you're pressured to meet deadlines, or you have to rush to catch a plane. You confront many frustrating domestic and social demands. Stress is brought about by money and personal problems, overcrowding, unrelenting noise, anxiety about inflation, fuel shortages, crime, war, and... well, you get the picture.

Coping with these kinds of problems requires you to use your head rather than your fists, but your body prepares for "fist" action anyway. The cerebral cortex of the brain sees a threat and signals the hypothalamus, which switches on the nervous and endocrine systems. The nervous system in turn stimulates the liver, which increases the blood's clotting ability (reducing the likelihood of your bleeding to death should you be injured). Fat stored in the body is readied for conversion into energy. The heart rate speeds up to send extra oxygen to the muscles. Muscle tension increases to facilitate quick responses. Large amounts of hormones are released to allow the body to engage in long periods of intense activity. All this happens automatically in response to a threat, whether it's real or imagined.

Today this physical response to threats is outmoded. After all, we're "civilized." In most instances, we hide our natural responses because fighting or running away is inappropriate. We learn to mask anger and bottle up our frustrations and anxieties. The natural, physical response is thwarted, and this causes more tension.

This results in a tremendous energy drain. It can ultimately lead to a high blood pressure and dangerous changes in blood chemistry. What can these lead to? You name it: obesity; ulcers; colitis; muscle twitches and tics; high blood pressure; heart disease; cancer; emotional disorders such as neurosis, anxiety, depression, and various compulsions. They're all there, the host of 20th-century maladies we have all come to know and live with—and fear. Each of these ailments, physical and emotional, can cause more tension. The cycle whirls and widens.

So get off the cycle: walk. Walking can release tension, provide an outlet for pent-up emotions, and release hormones and blood fats that would be harmful if contained in the body.

George Trevalyan, the famous historian, said, "I never knew a man to go for an honest day's walk for whatever distance, great or small...and not have his reward in the repossession of the soul."

Exercise experts agree that release of nervous tension is one of the most important functions of walking. They've been saying it for years. Simple rest can be beneficial in times of stress, but voluntary activity is even better. If you are embroiled in a particularly knotty problem and feel you need a break, it is better to walk or do some other form of exercise than simply sit back and do nothing. The physical exertion of walking will absorb your stress like a sponge.

The effectiveness of walking on reducing tension has been measured in the laboratory. A study conducted at the University of Southern California examined a group of men 50 years of age and over. All had a history of migraine headaches. The study found that after a few weeks of regular physical activity, the headaches disappeared—without medication. (As you may know, the accepted theory about migraines is that they are somehow caused by tension.)

A second USC study showed that a 15-minute walk reduced neuromuscular tension more effectively than did a standard dosage of tranquilizers. The researchers concluded that exercise can be more relaxing than medication.

The question is: How does walking reduce tension? There are several theories. It may just be escape—from big problems like international conflicts as well as smaller hassles such as the telephone, the children, parents, and occupational frustrations.

Walking is a mini-vacation—a vacation in the middle of the day, in the evening, or in the morning. It's a vacation that no one can take away from you. You don't have to worry about a thing. Your vacation can be short or quite long. You're free.

LESS ANXIETY, LOWER BLOOD PRESSURE

Anxiety is closely related to tension. No one knows exactly how they are related, but doctors know there is a connection. It's like the chicken and the egg: no one knows which came first. A lot of people are in fitness classes because they are too anxious. Their doctors realize that activity can reduce anxiety, so they recommended exercise.

Infrequent anxiety does little harm. But constant anxiety can cause problems. One of those problems is hypertension, a debilitating condition of high blood pressure that can be fatal if not checked. And it *can* be checked—with exercise. People whose lives were once defined by high blood pressure, anxiety, and a morbid fear of heart attacks have been transformed by a regular program of exercise. Their blood pressure has dropped dramatically and they no longer have unreasonable fears of death. They enjoy life. Such success stories are not flukes; similar results have been proved over and over again in strictly supervised tests. Walking and other forms of exercise (calisthenics, running, cycling, swimming) have benefited men and women of all ages.

Walking or exercise alone will not alleviate all cases of hypertension. But one thing is clear: it often does produce excellent results. (It works best for people who are overly anxious.) However, no one ought to begin an exercise program on a do-it-yourself basis to relieve a hypertensive condition. Anyone with high blood pressure should get medical clearance before engaging in increased physical activity—even walking.

Psychologists and psychiatrists have made exercise part of anxiety therapy. Results have been encouraging because exercise is a suitable outlet for the physical changes brought about by anxious feelings. Anxiety is reduced further during exercise because the patient gains a sense of accomplishment and achievement. For many people, physical exertion is associated with excitement, assertiveness, and friendship. These positive feelings may also help to relieve feelings of anxiety.

The standard medical concept, "Action absorbs anxiety," says it all.

RELIEF FROM DEPRESSION

Exercise also seems to help short-circuit depression. The term depression is a catch-all which may include everything from the blahs to psychosis. Depression is a serious problem in our society. Doctors tell us that over 10 percent of the population will score in the "depressed" range on what is known as a depression questionnaire. Some hospitals are reporting that over half the patients coming to their clinics list depression as their primary problem.

Doctors are now excited by reports that seem to show that exercise, such as walking, can relieve a person's depression. Although most of the studies to date have been done on running, we believe the conclusions can be extended to walking as well. Anything that is repetitive in nature, that allows people to relax, and gives them a feeling of accomplishment seems to be helpful in reducing depression. Here are several reasons why.

1. Walking regularly requires patience. A person learns through walking that it takes time to make significant physical changes. An appreciation of the value of patience may reduce depression.

2. Walkers learn, often dramatically, that they can change themselves for the better. They see that they are sufficiently in control of their lives to be able to improve their health, appearance, and self-image.

3. In this way they develop a feeling of accomplishment. Any time you experience a sense of success, you will probably be pulled out of depression.

There's an old comedy routine about a doctor who steps on his patient's foot to make the patient forget about his headache. There's something of that in the relationship between walking and depression. Walkers are forced to notice new and significant body sensations, which distract them. People who walk tend to focus on their sore calves or other muscle groups and forget about the annoying physical symptoms of depression.

These changes can make walking almost addictive. Many people find they need their walk as much as others need their morning cup of coffee. Walkers transform a negative addiction into a positive one. They start to give up such things as smoking, drinking, overeating, and nonproductive arguing.

WALKING TO EUPHORIA

If you talk to long-distance runners, they'll tell you about the euphoria they experience after running 30 or 40 minutes. It's called a "runner's high." Many people who have participated in walking programs have experienced the same kind of thing by seeing their world at three to four and a half miles an hour. They feel a period of heightened consciousness; they feel more creative, enthusiastic, excited. Some psychologists feel that this "high" is an altered state of consciousness, an opening up of the unconscious.

Thought processes are altered. Problems seem to become less important and many are let go. It's almost as if there were a psychiatrist inside of you, helping you solve your problems as you walk.

Some experts have tried to show that exercise and walking improve circulation; that this improved circulation sends the brain more oxygen, which brings on the euphoria. This is often expressed as better productivity at work, and less absenteeism. The mind is opened up by the body's exposure to fresh air and scenery. You have a chance to work things out in your own mind. New ideas to help you solve old problems are likely to pop into your head while you walk. This does not seem likely to occur while you watch TV or worry. Here's our advice: When you can't solve a problem, go for a walk!

Slowing Down the Aging Process

Have you ever known a person in his forties or fifties who looks—and acts—decades older? Someone who is sedentary, overweight or underweight, depressed, physically stooped? Chances are that you do know such a person. They have allowed their middle age to become *old* age.

Middle age, it has been said, is the time when the narrow waistline and the broad mind change places. That's clever, but not very amusing. There's no way that any of us can avoid growing old. But we can do something to assure that we'll age gracefully and continue to enjoy life to the fullest every day: exercise.

Many changes occur as we get older. Among the most common are fatigue, decreased vigor and strength, increased weight, reduced joint flexibility, a change in bowel and bladder habits, a decline in sex drive, failing sight and hearing, a decrease in mental agility, and general lack of stamina.

The process of aging varies a great deal from one person to another. It's impossible to determine the exact time of life when it will begin. We usually associate aging with the age of 65 or so, but the signs begin to appear in most of us as early as 30 or 35 years of age. Some people seem washed out before the age of 40. On the other hand, we all know people who seem young and vigorous at 60 or 70 years of age.

Although the average American probably assumes that the changes that occur after the age of 30 are a natural part of the aging process, this is probably incorrect. Current research suggests that such change may be the result not of passing years, but a passive life style. For example, Swedish researchers placed five healthy young men in bed for 20 days. After the bed rest, the researchers found that the maximum cardiac output of the men decreased 26 percent, their maximum oxygen uptake dropped 27 percent, and their exercise stroke volume and maximum breathing capacity fell 30 percent. Even their amount of lean body tissue decreased.

The phenomena of aging are the reverse of those caused by exercise training. In some populations, a decrease in the amount of habitual exercise accentuates several "age" changes; in others with lifelong exercise, the state of training delays them. Long-term exercise may have a positive effect on health, even if it does not prolong life. Such an effect would be manifested by a lower frequency of illness throughout one's life.

The later years of life—particularly those of retirement—should be happy, dynamic years. The retirement years can be truly rewarding, if you have energy and vitality. But the promise of a full life in our later years comes only to those who are healthy, alert, robust, and active. Unfortunately for too many Americans, the dream of a happy, healthy retirement never comes true.

Most people make financial plans for their retirement. They have financial resources they hope will ensure happiness. However, many have neglected their physical resources. By the time they are 60, their stamina has faltered, their weight has escalated, and their general health has declined. Suddenly, their financial resources are no longer as important as they once were. The concern for wealth gives way to concern for health.

Your body inevitably changes with time. Walking will not keep you young, but it can slow down the natural aging process, and lengthen the middle-age plateau. You will not grow old before your time. Granted, slowing the aging process in middle age and maintaining the body longer at that level is not the mythical fountain of youth, but it's the next best thing.

Walking is safe for people who are in their later years. Walking programs can be tailored to individual needs and fitness levels. It is important to heed the advice of your doctor, but just as important to pay attention to your body's own barometer as you walk. When you become fatigued, slow your pace. If you aren't exerting yourself at all, *increase* your pace. When your pulse rate increases and you exert yourself to the point of slight breathlessness, you'll condition and improve your cardiovascular system. You don't have to be afraid to walk just because you're getting older. You might have slowed down a bit and lost a little flexibility over the years, but that doesn't mean you have to live like a recluse. All you have to do is take it easy at the start, listen to your doctor, and listen to your body.

Many older people who have suffered severe heart attacks or other ailments have firmed their resolve and begun to walk. Some even run. With the advice of their physicians, such people have strengthened their bodies, improved their mental outlook, and regained their love of life.

CAN'T WALKING BE HARMFUL?

Since 1967 almost 1,000 people (85 percent of whom had diagnosed heart disease) have participated in the Cardiac Pulmonary Resuscitation Institute (CAPRI) Program of Seattle, Washington. Patients in the program walk fast or jog one hour a day, three times a week. In nine years there have been 15 incidents of patient collapse during exercise. (All were successfully resuscitated.) At first that may sound excessive. But the patients had logged over 116,000 hours of activity. That means that there was one collapse every 7,700 hours. Certainly, one collapse is still a serious matter. But those are still pretty good odds, and they look even better when you consider what the odds of the patients would have been had they not engaged in the program. Most of those people were headed for deadly heart attacks.

A 1975 Stanford University study of cardiac rehabilitation programs stated that one collapse can be expected in every 17,585 hours of rehabilitative exercise, and one fatal collapse every 94,957 hours. This means the risk of death for cardiac patients while exercising in a medically supervised exercise program is about the same as that reported for cardiac patients in general.

Research has shown that older people can withstand great amounts of exercise. In fact, since most of them were active during their childhood and young adult years (there were few automobiles or school buses back then), they have a good base. And they are able to pick up exercise quite well. Many, once conditioned, seem to have more stamina than the average teenager of today.

RECENT RESEARCH ON AGING

In recent years there has been an increase in research on the problems of aging. The studies state that the control of senescence—the fight against aging—should begin as early as possible, and exercise is an excellent way to do it. The heart, brain, regulatory functions, and the whole body benefit.

Studies of long-lived Russian peasants have found that many of these older people had forms of heart and blood vessel diseases, but the oxygen supply to their hearts was so good as a result of collateral circulation that heart attacks were unnoticed and did little harm. The collateral circulation (additional circulation caused by the opening of new blood vessels) is thought to be the result of an active life style. In other words, exercise didn't hurt them. And it won't harm you. You can walk without fear, provided you follow the principles outlined in this book.

A three-day conference on exercise and aging held at the National Institute of Health in Bethesda, Maryland, spelled out the relationship between exercise and aging.

1. Walking is the most efficient form of exercise— and the only one you can safely follow all the years of your life.

2. As people get older, their bones start to demineralize and lose their resistance to breaking. Exercise, such as walking, slows the bone demineralization process, particularly in the legs. Through exercise your bone-growing cells are stimulated. Bones remain tougher and less likely to break. This also promotes a greater range of motion.

(A Reno, Nevada, orthopedic clinic did extensive tests on a man, at least 60 years old, who has exercised vigorously for the past 12 years. The tests included x-rays of his legs. At the conclusion of their study, one of the doctors sent a letter to him which said, "Your bone age is approximately 12 years less than your chronological age. This indicates to me that your exercising has been effective in slowing the aging process.")

3. As people get older, particularly those who have smoked or who have worked in high-pollution areas, they develop emphysema-like changes in their lungs. Those individuals who exercise may still exhibit such changes, but they still have far greater capacity than sedentary people.

4. As you age, your cardiovascular function declines. It loses its elasticity and vigorousness. Yet the cardiovascular systems of older Americans who exercise show a maximum preservation of function.

5. One obvious phenomenon of aging is an increase in obesity. As people get into their 40s, 50s, and 60s, their weight escalates. So does their percentage of body fat. This condition greatly affects health. But exercise is a strong deterrent to obesity.

6. Closely related to obesity is the fact that as people get older they tend to eat less than they used to in an effort to keep their weight under control. When they do this, their nutrition often suffers. Daily exercise permits greater food intake and better blood circulation, which improves each cell's nourishment while preventing obesity.

7. Besides heart disease and cancer, many older Americans fear late-onset diabetes. Even though this disease can be controlled, it kills, maims, and reduces a person's

well-being. Interestingly, late-onset diabetes is almost entirely reversible by exercise if you are overweight.

8. Rheumatoid arthritis and osteoarthritis are common in older people. It has been estimated that over 90 percent of all Americans over the age of 60 have some form of osteoarthritis. The conference studies showed that arthritics can perhaps benefit the most of all older people from exercise—provided the exercise is increased slowly but steadily.

9. Many Americans fear getting older. They fear that they will be "turned out to pasture," become unwanted. This increases stress, depression, and fear. Walking seems to stem the tide. Exercise improves the quality of life. Research comparing exercise to a widely prescribed tranquilizer found exercise to be superior in relaxing and elevating one's mood—with none of the drug's side-effects.

In other words, experts and researchers on aging today see the wisdom in the statement that "walking is man's best medicine." That statement came from Hippocrates, the father of medicine, over 2,000 years ago.

Many older Americans today claim they are regimented, merely tolerated by society rather than being considered vital and valued members of it. One excellent way to escape that regimentation is by taking part in what we call the fitness revolution. Choose to walk while everyone else is riding. Go for a nice vigorous walk when everyone else is cemented to an easy chair. Condition your body while others let theirs go to pot. When you get into the real spirit of the revolution, you can always dream up your own personal ways of showing your physical individuality. And you'll find that you've never had more fun.

If you're going to break out of your sedentary rut for good, you will have to get rid of the excuses for not exercising. But, of course, it must be done carefully and thoughtfully. Enthusiasm should be directed to the goal of moving closer to fitness every day, not to setting records. Don't let your enthusiasm trick you into overdoing it.

Starting a walking program with a 10-mile hike is foolish. Do most exercises gently, being careful not to put too much stress on your legs and ankles.

Inserting a new activity into your life means that you may have to leave something else out. You need to take stock of your priorities. When you stop to think about it, how many things are more important than your health and well-being?

A few years ago a man we know found an interesting solution to what could be a problem for many older walkers. He began by walking to and from work every day, a distance of several miles. Much of the route took him along a narrow country road. In late autumn, the early sunset made it necessary for him to walk home in the dark, which made his wife nervous. On the verge of giving up his walking, he did some thinking and realized he could walk to work in the morning, then walk home at noon and get his car. A fitness problem was licked in a simple and obvious way.

The old saying "It's never too late" certainly applies to walking. It is one of the best ways to break out of the sedentary rut. Just start your mind working in the right direction; your legs will follow right along.

If you begin exercising as we've suggested, will you live to be 100? Probably not; yet you do have a better chance of reaching that age if you do exercise than you have if you don't. Exercise will put you in better physical condition. It can slow the aging process—sometimes by many years. And it makes you feel younger. With these benefits, how can you lose?

Your
Walking Program

You acquired your walking skills when you were between the ages of nine months and two years, so you don't need anyone to tell you how to walk. Although this chapter will lay out some specific instructions that we believe you ought to follow in order to maximize the benefits of a walking program, the "secret" of walking comfortably is to walk naturally—pretty much as you've been walking up to now.

Yet the program we've developed for you amounts to more than a leisurely stroll. To continue to enjoy the rewards of this program, you may eventually find yourself walking for more than an hour, several days a week. Our program allows you to start slowly and progress without strain. However, because we know that some of you will be impatient and will be tempted to push yourselves too hard, we'd like you to answer this question before you go any further: Do you have any questions about your health?

If you do, check with your doctor before you start your walking program. Of course, if you have arthritis, anemia, low back pain, uncontrolled diabetes, or serious diseases of the lungs, kidneys, liver or heart, you ought to be seeing a doctor regularly anyway. But many Americans have a tendency to take their health for granted and allow too much time to elapse between physical examinations.

Those of you who have questions about your health should get a check-up. That check-up should include an examination of your heart, blood vessels, muscles, and joints. Ideally, your blood would be analyzed for cholesterol and triglycerides, and your blood pressure would be noted. A resting electrocardiogram (ECG) should also be performed.

In some cases, it may be a good idea to take an exercise stress test, which is nothing more than an electrocardiogram that is taken while you are exercising.

It is generally agreed in the medical community that, if you are under 30, you can start exercising if you've had a check-up in the past year and your doctor found nothing wrong with you. If you are between 30 and 39, you should have a check-up within three months of the time you start exercising, and the examination should include an electrocardiogram (ECG) taken at rest. If you are between 40 and 59, your guidelines are the same as those for the 30–39 group, plus an ECG taken while you are exercising. And if you are over 59, you should follow the age 40–59 requirements, with the examination taking place immediately before you embark on any exercise program.

But an examination (with or without a stress test) isn't the final answer. Let's face it, not all doctors understand exercise. Some have negative attitudes about it. So here is some further advice. Before following your doctor's advice on exercise, check these things out:

1. Look at your physician's waistline. If it seems too big, don't trust his exercise advice.

2. Make sure your doctor is a nonsmoker.

3. Find out if he is taking part in an aerobic exercise program; that is, exercising three or more times a week. (Golf does not qualify.)

If he passes these three hurdles, then tell him you are going to participate in a walking program. Show him this book, referring to this chapter. Then ask the following:

1. Can you clear me for participation in this program?

2. How long, how hard, and how often am I permitted to exercise?

If your doctor realizes you're serious about exercising, he or she should be pleased. But if he or she reacts with a comment like "Remember, if you walk one mile from home you'll have to walk one mile back," get a second opinion from another doctor.

Doctors deal with sickness, not well-being, so they tend to think in negative rather than positive terms. Don't forget, it's your health. You want to make sure what you're doing is right. You want to obtain the best advice available.

After your doctor has given you the go-ahead, you may become concerned about proper walking style. The best advice is to walk naturally. Your body is unique. It has its own particular construction and balance, so you can't force it to behave exactly like someone else's.

It is good to keep your spine straight and hold your head high as you walk, but try not to be so conscious of this that you feel unnatural. Don't exaggerate your arm motion. Allow your arms to hang loosely at your sides. They will swing in the opposite action of your legs. Keep your hands, hips, knees, and ankles relaxed. As you walk, don't worry about the length of your stride. Just do whatever is comfortable. Each foot should strike the ground at your heel. The weight is then transferred from your heel up along the outer border of your foot toward your toes. Then you should push off with your toes to complete the foot strike pattern. As you move from heel to toe, you will get a rolling motion. Avoid landing flat-footed and on the balls of your feet. If you do, you may be headed for some leg and foot problems later on.

When walking, breathe naturally. If you feel comfortable with your mouth closed, close it. If it seems better open, then open it. Remember, the faster you go the more air you'll need. Help yourself to all the air you want.

Don't follow these guidelines slavishly. It's likely that the way you walk already is best for you. Remember, you're not in a beauty contest. You're walking for fitness and fun. There's no need to worry about style or form.

THREE MORE IMPORTANT PRINCIPLES

There are three other principles you ought to follow as you walk.

First, you should be able to hold a conversation with someone beside you as you go. Even when you walk alone, you can use your imagination: do you feel like talking? If not, you can probably conclude that you're walking too fast for your present age or fitness level. This is called the talk test. The talk test is especially important during the first six to 12 weeks of walking.

Second, your walk should be painless. If you experience any chest, jaw, or neck pain, you should slow down. If this doesn't stop the pain, see your doctor and describe what happened. Try to recall the circumstances: "I was walking on a hill," "It occurred during the first few minutes," or "The weather was cold."

Third, if after walking you seem excessively tired for an hour or longer, the walk was too strenuous. Next time, walk slower and not as far. Your walk should be exhilarating; not fatiguing. If you experience a dizzy or lightheaded feeling, or if your heart is beating too fast while you walk, it's time to back off. If you have a strange hollow feeling in your chest, feel like vomiting, or are tired for at least a day after walking, take it easy. If you can't sleep at night or if your nerves seem shot, it means that you've been pushing too hard. The same is true if you seem to have lost your zing or can't get your breath after a few minutes of exercise. These are your body's warning signs.

All three points emphasize "listening to your body." This listening is something you'll have to learn. But you'll probably find it fun. You'll enjoy your body more. It will let you know when to slow down and when to speed up. You are the best judge of your exercise.

As we have said before, the health of your heart and lungs are critical to your overall well-being. The cells in your body need oxygen to live and grow. Without enough of it, they die. Your lungs take in oxygen and give it to the blood. Your heart pumps blood and the oxygen it is carrying to the cells in your body. The cells take the oxygen from the blood and "burn" it as fuel to grow and work. Anytime something is burned, carbon dioxide is produced. The blood removes this carbon dioxide from your cells; your lungs then send it out into the air.

This process goes on all the time. If your lungs and heart are working properly, you look and feel great. But if your lungs can't take in enough oxygen or if your heart can't pump blood fast enough, your cells can be crippled or killed. This is why any worthwhile physical fitness program must focus on the heart and lungs and how they work together. According to the American Heart Association's Committee on Exercise and Fitness, and the American College of Sports Medicine, an exercise contributes to heart and lung fitness only if it continuously involves both systems for at least 15 minutes or, preferably, 20 minutes or more. That is why a game of tennis, even a very active one, is not the most useful exercise to strengthen the heart and lungs. There may be periods of furious activity, full of lunging and running and rapid stops and starts. But they are too short, and there is too much rest in between. The action is not sustained. Walking, on the other hand, is sustained. It is rhythmical and continuous. This is why it also burns a significant number of calories thus helping to control weight and reduce body fat.

The best walking program is one based on the principles of sustained action. The amount of time spent walking (the amount of sustained action), not the distance or pace, is the crucial consideration.

Most people measure exercise in terms of time, distance, physical load, or number of actions. Few people think about effort. Effort and work don't mean the same thing. Two people may walk a mile in 15 minutes. Both walk the same distance. But for one person the walk may be effortless, while the other one finds that it is all he can handle. You may be like that second person. If you walk consistently, however, soon walking a mile in 15 minutes won't be difficult at all. Your body will have become more efficient, so you will need less effort to walk the same distance.

So how can you know how much exercise is right? For that matter, how can a program tell you? Your body is not like anyone else's, and it changes from day to day. According to many experts, a computer would be needed to figure out how much activity a particular person needs to benefit from the training effect. Most experts believe that you have a computer built into your body. It's your heart. By exercising at a specific heart rate, you maintain a consistent level of effort. Since your heart reacts to your general condition on a particular day, it will reflect your fatigue, body temperature, and other conditions when you exercise.

USING YOUR HEART RATE AS A GUIDE

Everyone has what is called a "maximum heart rate." Your maximum heart rate is the number of beats your heart makes per minute when you are running as far, as fast, and as long as possible. (Another term for this is maximum aerobic power level.) Although it varies from person to person, your maximum heart rate is roughly 220 minus your age. If you are 20 years old, your maximum heart rate is about 200; if you are 40, it is about 180.

There is no need for you to exercise at your maximum heart rate level. This could even be dangerous. Fortunately, physiologists have figured out a safe heart range for most people. They call this your target heart rate. Your target heart rate, as it is called in cardiovascular exercise programs, is considered about 70 to 85 percent of your maximum heart rate. That is your optimum level for exercise. That doesn't mean that you can't improve your fitness if your heart rate is above or below this range. It's just that the 70 to 85 percent range is the safest, most efficient range.

If you are **age 20**, your maximum heart rate is **200** beats per minute, and your target heart rate (75 percent of your maximum) is **150**. In other words, 150 heartbeats per minute is, on average, the safest and most beneficial number of beats for a 20-year-old during exercise. That person's target heart rate *range* may be anywhere from **140** to **170** beats per minute, but 150 is the ideal number.

If you are **age 30**, your maximum heart rate is **190**, and your target heart rate is **142**. Your heart rate range may be **133** to **162**.

If you are **age 40**, your maximum heart rate is **180**, and your target heart rate is **135**. Your heart rate range may be **126** to **153**.

If you are **age 50**, your maximum heart rate is **170**, and your target heart rate is **127**. Your heart rate range may be **119** to **145**.

If you are **age 60**, your maximum heart rate is **160**, and your target heart rate is **120**. Your heart rate range may be **112** to **136**.

If you are **age 70**, your maximum heart rate is **150**, and your target heart rate is **112**. Your heart rate range may be **105** to **128**.

Calculating your target heart rate for your precise age is easy. If, for example, you are 55, your target heart rate is approximately 124, or the mid-point between the rates for people aged 50 and 60.

To obtain the cardiovascular benefits of walking—or of any other exercise—maintain a heart rate between 70 percent and 85 percent of your maximum (your approximate target heart rate) for at least 15, or preferably, 20 minutes. If you exceed 85 percent of your maximum rate, you are overdoing it and should relax your pace.

To use the preceding information, you must be able to take your pulse, that is, determine your heartrate. This is very easy.

There are three ways to take your pulse: at the radial artery on your wrist, the temporal artery on your forehead, and the carotid artery on your neck. To take your pulse at your wrist, use the second, third, and fourth fingers of your hand to feel for the pulse along the thumb side of your wrist. When you find your pulse (a thump or push) count it for 10 seconds by doing the following. Right before you actually start counting, count the beats by going zero, zero, zero. As soon as the second hand on your watch reaches 12, start counting. First count zero, then one, two, three, four, etc. Stop counting when the second hand reaches the two (10 seconds). Multiply the number you counted by six. The number you get is your pulse. (You can also take your pulse for six seconds and add a zero. This is the easiest and most convenient way, but it can be less accurate.) If you want to take your pulse at your forehead, simply place your third and fourth fingers on your forehead and press. The counting is the same as for the wrist pulse. If you find you can't find your pulse at your wrist or at the forehead, you may use the neck pulse. But if you do this, be careful. Physicians and exercise physiologists frown upon taking a pulse this way. When people place their fingers at their neck, they may develop heart arrthymias (irregular heart beats). Their pulse rates also may slow down and give a false reading. So if you take your pulse this way, be sure to press lightly.

You now know your target heart rate and how to take your heart rate. The next step is learning how to keep your heart rate in the proper range when walking. The only way you can do this is by going out and walking. At first you will have to experiment a little, but after a while you will be able to tell whether you are within the range simply by the way you feel.

If you tire quickly and noticeably when you walk within your target heart rate range, reassess your range and lower it. Slow down until you are still working hard but not overexerting yourself. If, on the other hand, you do not feel the effect of your walking, you may have to walk at a faster rate.

A word of caution: Don't be a slave to your pulse rate. Remember the three principles outlined at the beginning of this chapter.

Your maximum heart rate (or maximum aerobic power level) is a difficult measurement to obtain. It requires a great deal of sophisticated equipment, a medical doctor or exercise physiologist, and healthy chunks of time and money. But an accurate reading of your own pulse will give you a good approximation of your maximum aerobic power. Since you can find it without much trouble, you have an easy, inexpensive tool for measuring how strenuously you are exercising.

HOW TO GET STARTED

Doctors know that most sedentary people develop orthopedic problems by trying to do too much too soon. It is also known that most people who have had heart attacks while exercising had them within the first few weeks. The problem seems to be an effort to do too much too soon. Some doctors say you should spend at least one month reconditioning yourself for every year you have been sedentary. That's excellent advice.

You need a plan that puts you on a regular walking schedule. We're now going to take you step-by-step through a program that works. It has been tested and perfected over the past five years and has been used by thousands of people all over the United States and Canada. It will make you fit and help you enjoy the true pleasures of walking. You'll find this program demanding enough to get the job done, yet flexible enough to be adapted to your particular needs, age, present level of fitness, and life style.

Don't let the idea of an exercise program scare you off. We won't ask you to do more than you can reasonably do. We just want you to get started, and to keep at it. We want to help you experience the physical, mental, spiritual exhilaration of walking. All the benefits we have described are waiting for you.

There are two Starter Programs, designated A and B. Starter Program A is designed for those people who find that, as they walk, their heart rate is below their target zone. Using this program, you walk at a pace that does not elicit a target heart rate. All you do is walk comfortably and pain-free. You goal at this point is to get your body ready for more demanding exercise. You can elect to walk either four or six times a week; if four times a week, you will gradually increase your walking time from 20 minutes to 45 minutes, in increments of 5 minutes. It is best to stay at each time level for one week, but don't hesitate to stay two weeks at any level if that feels comfortable to you. Always listen to your body.

If you choose to exercise six times a week, you will begin with 15-minute walks, and progress—week-by-week— to walks of 17, 20, 23, 26, and 30 minutes. Again, if you wish to stay at one particular level longer than one week, do so.

If you find that you reach your target heart rate range even when you walk at a fairly slow pace, you should try Starter Program B. With this program, you will walk three or four times a week, beginning with 10 minutes and working your way up to walks of 12, 14, 16, 18, and 20 minutes. If the 10 minutes a day three or four times a week seems too difficult (if you are out of breath, etc.), walk only five minutes or less each time. Some emphysema patients walk only one minute at the start. You must be the judge.

Some people may think the Starter Program is too basic, not hard enough. We don't agree. Most people "attack" a fitness program, and after a few weeks, they quit. Remember, your primary purpose should be to get motivated to exercise on a regular basis and keep at it. Anybody can start an exercise program, but not everyone can stay at it. So follow these directions and stay with one of the Starter Programs. Do not jump ahead.

Do not worry about the speed of your walks. Just walk for time. As you walk, you may want to take your pulse. If it's below your target heart rate range, that's all right for the Starter Program. If it exceeds your target heart rate range, slow down. And don't worry about the number of miles you cover. Most people will cover a mile in 20 minutes; some will be slower, and some faster. Mileage is not important.

MAKING PROGRESS

Once you complete the Starter Program, you are ready for bigger and better things. Now it's time to progress to the Advanced Walking Program. Like the Starter Program, the Advanced Program is divided into Program A and Program B.

dvanced Program A is for people whose heart
their target heart rate range when they walk. It is
that participants in Advanced Program A have
gressed through Starter Programs A and B.
be taken three or four times a week, and will
minutes, rising gradually (one week at a time is
minutes. Two-minute increments will be the
tween 22 and 30 minutes (22, 24, 26, etc.),
-minute increments will mark your progress
minutes to 60 minutes (30, 33, 36, 39, etc.).
er that these levels are only guidelines. If at any
the exercise seems excessive or your body is rebelling,
back. Spend a minimum of one week at each level.

If your heart rate is below your target heart rate range as you walk, you are ready for Advanced Program B. On this program, you will walk four or six times a week. If four times, you will gradually progress from 50-minute walks to walks lasting 120 minutes. Progress will be made in five-minute increments. Spend a minimum of one week at each level.

If you will be walking six times a week, you will begin with 33-minute walks and gradually progressing to walks lasting 80 minutes. Progress will be made in increments of three and four minutes: 33, 36, 40, 43, 47, 50, 53, 57, 60, 63, 67, 70, 73, 77, and 80 minutes.

Some people who choose to walk only four times a week find that the two hours of walking required by the final level is a little too much. So we advocate going 80 minutes six times a week. Also, our experience with walkers shows that when you are not walking at target heart rate levels, four times a week or more—not three— seems to be the best number of days to exercise.

How far you progress depends on your fitness goals. If you want to improve your physical fitness levels, concentrate on the first third of whichever Advanced Program you choose. If you are interested in weight control and percentage of body fat, concentrate on the midpoint of your program. If you wish to reduce cholesterol and triglycerides, concentrate on the second third of your program. And if you wish to experience feeling of euphoria, concentrate on your prog third.

Walking will allow your heart rate to re target range. Of course, as you improve, you m faster to keep it at that level. Most of you can't along and expect to reach 70 to 85 percent of maximum heart rate. You'll have to walk at a good c that is uncomfortable, use Program B. Here you v longer at a lower pulse rate. This is especially beneficial the person who is just beginning to exercise after a lor layoff.

The following is a good rule of thumb. If you are unable to work at your target level, double the number of minutes you walk. For example, if you want to do 30 minutes of target heart rate exercise and find that you can't get your heart rate up that high, go to 60 minutes or more. It's a fair compromise. And that's exactly what the two walking programs are. They have been adjusted so that you can walk at a level suitable for you. Just remember: listen to your body.

How long and how often you walk depends upon your fitness objectives.

If you're interested in improving your fitness level, you should walk at 70 to 85 percent of your maximum heart rate for at least 20 minutes (15 minutes in a pinch) three times a week. As you start to improve, you may want to work up to about 30 minutes.

If you want to lose weight and fat, walk at 70 to 85 percent of your maximum heart rate for 30 minutes or longer at least four times a week.

If you want to reduce coronary heart disease risk factors like cholesterols and triglycerides (increase the number of high-density lipoproteins), walk at 70 to 85 percent of your maximum heart rate for 30 to 45 minutes or more, four or more times a week.

To help yourself mentally reduce depression and anxiety, work at 70 to 85 percent of your maximum for 45 minutes to an hour, three or more times a week.

To reduce blood pressure, the answer is not quite as clear. But the best advice seems to be: Don't worry so much about target heart rates unless you can exercise at that level comfortably. Exercise slowly for at least 30 minutes, five or more times a week.

WHEN TO WALK AND WHAT TO WEAR

Listen to your biological clock. Don't try to force yourself into a mold. It won't work. Be specific. Know yourself. If you're an owl, exercise in the evening. If you're a lark, do it in the morning. If the afternoon is your time of day, do it then. Whatever time is appropriate, make sure to give yourself a time commitment. You must be willing to set aside a certain period of time each day or every other day. At first a little experimenting may be necessary to find out what works best for you.

But whatever you do, don't worry about taking the time. You're doing something positive for your body, and it will make you feel better—more productive and more alive. All you are taking is about 4 percent of your day.

The most important equipment you will own when walking are your shoes. You can cover just as much territory in old cut-off shorts and a T-shirt as you can in an expensive designer's outfit. But a good pair of shoes spell the difference between pain and comfort—success and failure.

Your feet take a lot of punishment when you walk and protecting them helps you avoid injuries. When they first begin, walkers think any old shoe will do. They are convinced the expensive running shoes are overrated. This is not so. If you follow this advice, you'll walk without pain. Good shoes are essential. (Of course, there are exceptions. The mountain people of the Andes have gnarled feet that are exceptionally wide. Their feet have so many blood vessels that they are almost immune to the cold. They can walk barefoot on the snow! They can walk for long periods of time across rocky crevices, extremely hard trails, and knife-sharp rocks. But most of us have tender feet.)

Walkers tend to have the same kind of foot problems that runners have. When they use tennis or basketball shoes, they're headed for trouble. Once a person starts to go beyond a half hour of walking daily, he needs a shoe that gives good support. Some people encounter problems at lower levels. So if you're serious about fitness and are going to walk, get a good pair of running shoes. You might ask: Why running shoes for walking? The answer is simple. Running shoes provide the support, protection, comfort, and cushioning that your feet will need for walking on all kinds of surfaces. And you do need support for all the walking you'll be doing. Each mile you walk, your foot hits the ground about 400 times. In a four-mile walk, that's about 1,600 times. If you weight 200 pounds, each foot receives a total impact of 320,000 pounds—or 160 tons. That's a lot of pounding on your feet, legs, and hips. You'll need support for your feet. You're going to need shoes which will cost you between $20 and somewhat more than $40.

The Right Shoes

Your feet will probably be two of the first parts of your body to feel the ill effects of poor walking technique because of their proximity to the ground.

Think about the shoes you're wearing now, or the ones you'll put on tomorrow. Unless they're brand-new, you probably don't notice how they feel on your feet, since they don't pinch or rub you the wrong way. But do you think you could walk a couple of miles in them without suffering? If you've ever had to walk long distances without advance warning (your car broke down on a lonely stretch of road, or you mistakenly got out of the cab at the wrong airline terminal), you know how painful it can be to walk in shoes that do not fit exactly right.

In this chapter we discuss five types of shoes: the conventional "fashion" shoe like the ones you probably wear to work; the once-popular shoe with the "negative-heel" design; hiking boots; some new shoes designed especially for people who walk a great deal; and running shoes. We believe running shoes are best for use by persons following a specific walking program.

Those of you who decide to walk to and from work as part of your walking program may not want to wear running shoes and carry your work shoes as you walk. You might try to walk in your work shoes. Is this all right?

It *is* if you are walking comfortably in your shoes—no matter what the style—and not experiencing any blisters, irritation, pain, or fatigue. But if you *are* experiencing problems, you must exercise great care when you look for a new pair.

Ideally, the shoes you select should have cushioning, such as crepe soles. The cushioned sole lessens the shock that travels up the legs when walking on concrete. Make sure you can wriggle your toes a bit. Your foot should not slide from side to side, but neither should there be tightness at the edges of your foot. The back side of the heels—the heel counter—should support the heel firmly. The shoe's sole should flex at the ball of the foot; if it does not, you will strain your Achilles tendon. On the other hand, the sole should not flex in the mid-part.

Remember to avoid excessively "stylish" shoes with narrow, cramping toes or heels higher than one-half to three-quarters of an inch above the soles.

Real leather is best, as it allows the foot to breathe. When being fitted, be sure to stand as well as sit. An oxford-type shoe with laces will be more comfortable and secure than a slip-on.

Don't forget that even the finest pair of shoes cannot correct structural problems in your feet. See a doctor or podiatrist if you believe you have foot or toe problems.

Shoes with negative heels—once very popular— are no longer as widely seen. In any case, experts disagree on the consequences of wearing such shoes. Individual heel, arch, and posture requirements will dictate the suitability of such shoes for you. If in doubt, see your doctor.

Any shoe—particularly negative-heel shoes—require some breaking in. That means two to four weeks of adjustment, a gradual increase in wearing time: one hour the first day, and one hour added every one to three days. During this period, you may have heel pain and mild stiffness or cramps in the calves. Don't be discouraged this early in the game. But if you still feel the sensation after one month's time, take the hint. The negative-heel shoe may not be for you.

So far we've discussed only the shoes that would be used by persons who walk in urban or suburban areas.

But what about those of you who may wish to do your walking in the bush? Hiking boots are a necessity. Some people have walked to the tops of mountains in running shoes, but we can't recommend that. If you plan to do any strenuous hiking, you should choose boots, and choose them carefully.

Although all hiking boots tend to look pretty much alike, they can vary significantly. Pay attention to the total weight of the boot. For the average male, boots should weight about four to five pounds; for the average female, about a half pound less. If the boots are too light, your feet may get banged up. If your boots are too heavy, your legs will suffer from lifting unnecessary extra pounds hour after hour. Generally, if you're going to walk on the road, through the bush, and up mountains, the most versatile model will be what is called medium-weight hiking (or trail) boot. It may also be called a lightweight climbing boot. (Be wary of "climbing boots": they may not be suitable for prolonged walking.)

Boots should have a hard toe, a rubber-lug sole, padding around the instep and ankle, and uppers that reach at least two inches above your ankle. The upper should be made of good leather. The fewer the seams in the uppers, the more rugged the boot.

Find a store with a salesperson you feel you can trust. Ask a few questions. If you seem to be getting reasonable answers, you can proceed.

Once you've selected your boots, you'll have to spend some time breaking them in. Wear them around the house and on short walks prior to wearing them for any extended period of time. One week is not enough. It will take you a good month or more to break them in properly. The length of time is contingent upon how much you walk.

RUNNING SHOES: BEST FOR WALKING

Despite the name, running shoes are our recommendation for walkers. Although you may talk to serious runners who'll tell you that you don't have to worry about the quality of your shoes unless you intend to log many miles of walking or running each week, we don't agree. If you want to progress smoothly and without pain, invest in a good pair of running shoes. Cheap shoes may save you money, but high-quality shoes will save your feet.

When you begin to look for running shoes, you'll notice that most of them—actually about 60 percent—are imported. Certain lines are identified with selected chains of shoe stores throughout the United States.

The problem is you may not be able to find a store that carries the brand of shoe you really want. And if you live outside a metropolitan area or an area where running is not yet popular, you're likely to become frustrated.

Another possibility is a mail-order dealer. Although you will not be able to inspect or try out the shoes before buying them, in almost all cases you can return the shoes if you are not happy with them. Many people buy their shoes this way without problems. But you need to take a few precautions. Be sure to send tracings of your feet along with your size. Try the shoes on as soon as they arrive. Walk around the house for a time. If the fit is not right, or if there is some other feature that makes them impractical for your feet, send the shoes back immediately. Don't wear the shoes outdoors: you will not be able to return them.

Finding the right shoe can be a bit complicated. There are so many brands on the market that it's difficult to choose. Personal preference plays a big role. What works for one person may not work for another. It comes down to this: if the shoe you have works for you, stay with it. When problems occur, look for common-sense solutions.

The following are some general guidelines to consider when shopping for running-walking shoes. We believe you ought to familiarize yourself with these factors and how they can affect your walking comfort.

Fit. You, not the experts, will be wearing the shoes. So no matter how marvelous the design, if it isn't right for you, it's a waste of money. Your feet, like your fingerprints, are individual. You should make your selection with that in mind.

Begin by drawing an outline of your feet. Place each foot on a piece of paper and draw around it. (The lead of the pencil should follow the curvature of your instep.) Since one foot may be larger than the other, it's a good idea to trace both. When you go to the store, compare the bottom of each shoe to your tracing. How closely do the shoes conform to your feet? Are they wide enough across the ball and the toe? Are they long enough?

When trying on shoes, wear the socks that you will use when walking. If you plan to wear two pairs of socks, as many walkers do, wear both.

Check the toe area with special care. When you walk, your foot will slide forward inside the shoe. Allow about half an inch between your toe and the front of the shoe. Too snug a fit can cause undue pressure, blisters, black toes, and corns. Be sure that your toes have enough room to spread out a little bit. Cramped toes can cause problems.

Lacing. Currently there are three lacing patterns used in shoes. The most common is the U-throat or U-box, which is a full lacing pattern down to the toes in the shape of a U, much like the lacing pattern found on most dress shoes. The vamp, or bulcher, pattern runs across the instep area of the foot and does not go all the way down to the toes. Recently, some shoe manufacturers have emphasized the speed-lacing arrangement. Here the laces pass through plastic or metal rings so the lace does not snag on the material on the shoe's upper when they are being tied. Many U-box or bulcher patterns incorporate speed lacing.

Support. Because your foot hits the ground so many times during the course of a walk, good support is a must. Most shoes designed for walking or running offer some measure of support, but they may not be sufficient for you. If the arch support in an otherwise excellent shoe seems inadequate, you can add foam rubber supports yourself. These inserts are readily available. Good built-in support is preferable, however.

Weight. Ordinary running shoes vary considerably (up to 25 percent) in weight. Weight can be a factor if you plan to run, but it isn't an important consideration for walking.

Flexibility. This is one of the more important factors in judging a shoe. Many injuries are caused by shoes that are too stiff. Unless the sole bends easily, your feet will suffer. Bend the shoe back and forth to test pliabiliy. The foresole must flex. If the sole at the ball of the foot is too stiff, then the Achilles tendon will be overstressed. The stress occurs because the leg works hard to bend the sole at the ball of the foot. If you weigh 200 pounds or more, you'll want more cushioning than sole flexibility. A shoe should not be flexible at the midsole or under the arch. If it is, the bottom of the foot will suffer from lack of support, and plantar fasciitis (a strain or partial rupture of the ligament that runs from the ball to the heel of the foot) will result.

Sole. All soles are made of rubber. They vary greatly in design. The sole must provide protection and cushioning while remaining flexible—no easy thing to accomplish. Most manufacturers solve the problem by providing double soles: a tough outer layer to resist impact; and one or more softer layers inside to cushion the feet and absorb shocks. This combination is definitely better than either hard or soft soles alone.

There also are distinctive tread designs. The trend today is toward the "waffle" tread, which is a series of raised grippers designed to provide greater traction. A number of patterns including square, round, star-shaped, and triangular grippers are offered by different companies. Because the shock of impact is born by the grippers rather than by the whole foot, the waffle tread probably provides more cushioning than a flat tread. But pending further evidence, we believe that tread design is largely a matter of personal preference.

Heel. A moderately elevated heel is best. The shoe should place the heel of the foot higher than the front of the foot. Measure the forefoot thickness at the ball of the foot, and measure the shoe's heel height at the point of maximum thickness of the sole, where it meets the heel of the foot. *Runner's World* magazine says, "A shoe that has a forefoot sole thickness of 14mm should have roughly 26-29mm thickness in the heel area, or 12-16mm more in the heel than in the forefoot."

The shoe should hold the heel of the foot snugly without discomfort. Make sure that the top of the heel hits the back of your foot at a comfortable level. If it is too low, there will not be enough support; if it is extremely high, you may develop blisters or Achilles tendon problems. Compare the depth of the running shoe's heel with that of your regular shoes. The heel counter, the piece on the back of the shoe that supports the heel and Achilles tendon, should be firm and comfortable. The counter should be firm, and the heel tabs should be of adequate height to help stabilize the heel during contact with the ground. It should not be so high as to become a source of chafing itself. The heel width is measured at the widest point from one side of the ankle pad to the other.

Toe box. The toe box design is extremely important. When you're walking downhill, your feet are forced forward in the shoes, so there should be at least a half inch of space between the tip of the longest toe and the inside surface of the front of the shoe. Most importantly, the toe box should be high enough to allow the toes to move freely. If the toe box is too low, the tops of the shoes will rub the tops of the toes and cause black toenails, blisters, and other toe problems. The toe box height should be about 1.2 inches. The toe box height is usually measured about one inch back from the inside top of the shoe.

Uppers. The uppers are the part of the shoe that gives it its distinctive appearance. Resist the temptation to judge a shoe by its color or sportiness. Function is more important. The upper must be firm enough to stabilize the foot and soft enough on the inside so that it doesn't irritate the foot. Avoid shoes with thick seams that may chafe.

Uppers are made of nylon, leather, or combinations of materials. Usually, nylon uppers are the best because they are light, permit good air circulation, and are easy to clean. Leather is preferable if you plan to walk a lot in inclement weather.

If you can afford it, buy two pairs of shoes. You might prefer to have one pair for ordinary walking and one pair for bad-weather walking. The extra pair is really a luxury rather than a necessity, however.

It is important to purchase new shoes before the old ones are completely worn out. Wear the new ones on shorter walks to break them in. By the time your old ones are ready to be discarded, the new ones will be comfortable.

Special Problems

If you've read this far and still haven't decided to begin a walking program following the guidelines we've set up, it could be because you're concerned about some special problems.

In the past, people who'd had heart attacks, suffered from emphysema or arthritis, or were extraordinarily overweight were given medicine or put on diets and were told to take it easy. Today the situation is different. Doctors are now telling their patients to get some exercise. In particular, they are telling them to walk.

As we've said before, if you have questions about your health or are seeing a doctor regularly for specific problems, do not begin a walking program until you have received permission and specific instructions from your doctor. We think you should go ahead and ask about walking, no matter how serious your condition. Chances are, your doctor will allow you to begin, even if you have one of the special problems discussed in this chapter.

OBESITY

This is a serious problem throughout the developed (overdeveloped?) world. Between 20 and 50 percent of all Americans have too much fat. Recent studies in Canada indicate that as much as 75 percent of all Canadians worry about their present weight. Americans worry too. Obesity—being grossly, not just a few pounds, overweight—has become an increasing health problem in recent years. Many doctors and experts on obesity have felt that obese people either will not or should not exercise. But the phenomenal success of many obese people in walking programs has prompted some new thinking. Obese people probably will not lose weight through extremely strenuous physical activity; yet they can achieve excellent results through walking.

Let's examine some of the causes of obesity and the reasons why walking has been a successful means of helping obese people to lose weight.

Hunger is perhaps one of the most misunderstood words in our vocabulary. It refers to the craving for food that is usually associated with a number of unpleasant sensations. A person who has had no food for many hours will have stomach contractions, often called hunger pangs. This is the gnawing sensation that you experience at 11 in the morning if you skipped breakfast. Most of us, fortunately, have never known the severe pain of acute hunger suffered by millions of starving people around the world. Therefore, most of us do not understand true hunger.

Appetite is often confused with hunger. Appetite is the desire for a specific type of food, such as strawberries, milk, pizza, cookies. Your appetite determines the kind of food you eat.

Satiety means complete fulfillment—the absence of both hunger and appetite—even though food may be available.

The stomach does not control hunger. Even a person who has had part or all of his stomach removed will continue to feel hungry. Hunger is a response of the hypothalamus, a tiny part of the brain, to the fluctuating glucose level of the blood: the "glucostatic regulation of food intake."

In simple terms, according to the "glucostatic theory," when the blood glucose concentration falls too far, the part of the hypothalamus that signals satiety reduces its inhibiting effects on the part that controls the hunger sensation. An impulse is sent from the hypothalamus to the stomach. When the stomach gets the signal, stomach contractions begin. This causes the feeling of hunger. Although there are still missing links in this theory, there is more scientific evidence to support it than any other concept.

It is not known what determines either the size of the meal eaten or the sense of fullness after a meal. Scientists think that there are receptors of some type in the gastrointestinal tract that may trigger a nervous or hormonal mechanism, which in turn activates the hypothalamic satiety center. This process may be triggered by taste and smell, the number of fat deposits in the body, amino acid imbalance, glucose released by the liver, and glucagon (a protein that elevates blood glucose levels).

Calories (found only in proteins, fats, and carbohydrates) are essential, therefore, to satisfy hunger for any period of time. Bulk has very little to do with satisfying hunger. The sense of fullness that many people experience when they eat low-calorie or noncaloric foods may be caused by receptors in the gastrointestinal tract, but the feeling of fullness does not last long. This prompts the old saying that certain foods don't "stick to your ribs."

This is a serious indictment of noncaloric foods. People who use diet sodas, soups, crackers, cookies, etc., in an effort to reduce weight are just kidding themselves. They may lose weight at first, but their hunger will continue because of low glucose levels. As a result they will be continually hungry.

In one experiment, rats were given a certain amount of food over a period of time. Activity and diet were maintained at a constant level, and the rats were able to hold a steady weight. The researchers then changed 10 percent of the diet to noncaloric food that was very similar to diet foods used by people. When the new food contained 10 percent inert material (no calories), the rats ate approximately 10 percent more food. When the researchers raised the noncaloric portion to 20 percent, the animals ate 20 percent more food. This trend continued as the proportion of noncaloric food was increased. Finally, the animals literally ate themselves to death attempting to satisfy their appetites with low-calorie high-bulk foods.

The glucostatic theory explains why some foods satisfy hunger and others don't. It is still not clear why some people crave more food than others and seem to be hungry all the time, but there are several theories.

The Appestat Theory. Scientists call the feeding and satiety center of the hypothalamus the appestat. It is the regulator that controls appetite. This regulator seems to be set a little higher in some people than in others. The person whose appestat is set higher usually has greater difficulty in controlling weight. Although experiencing both hunger and satiety, the person with a high setting needs a little more food (glucose, to which all proteins, carbohydrates, or fats are eventually converted) to satisfy the satiety center, or appestat. Exactly why the appestat is sometimes set too high is not clear. Many scientists nevertheless feel that this theory provides perhaps one of the more logical explanations of why people gain weight.

In primitive cultures, human beings had to be physically active to survive. A high appestat setting was an advantage: a person with a higher setting experienced greater hunger and pursued food much more aggressively than a person with a lower setting. As a result, that person hunted down, ate, and stored more food so that his or her body had additional energy at hand and more body tissue. During periods when little or no food could be found, stored body fat and tissue provided sustenance until food was found. The person with the lower appestat setting had less stored energy and body tissue. (Of course, the person who remained physically active in the pursuit and preparation of food never became obese.)

In modern Western society, the situation is reversed. Vigorous physical activity is no longer required to obtain and prepare food, but we still have appestats. Nowadays, if you have a high appestat setting, you are at a disadvantage. The evolutionary instinct to eat more food so that you will be able to survive in a period of crisis continues to operate, but today you are likely to be underexercised. You don't burn up the excess calories, so you gain weight. And, unless you become marooned on a desert island, chances are slim that a nutritional crisis will occur in your lifetime. So the pounds continue to add up.

You can, of course, restrict your caloric intake, but you will experience a continual hunger, a hunger that is constantly stimulated by food ads on TV, billboards, magazines, and newspapers. Your appestat will demand that the hunger be satisfied. Since hunger is satisfied by increasing caloric intake, unless you are extremely strong-willed, practically any diet is doomed to failure.

The Psychological Theory. According to this theory, obesity and overweight are by-products of psychological problems or of conditioning. A researcher can cause a rat to overeat by punishing it if it does not. This kind of conditioning occurs in human beings, too. Many children eat and overeat in an effort to win their parents' approval, or in some cases to avoid punishment. Some well-meaning parents still believe that "a fat child is a healthy child" and expect their children to overeat. Also, some parents and other adults give children cookies or candy as a reward for good behavior, or to distract them from crying after a fall.

A child's first exposure to overeating often occurs very early in life; a baby's tears are often misinterpreted as hunger. Unfortunately, many adults thrust a bottle in the mouth of a crying infant instead of considering whether the need may be for cuddling, comfort, a change of diaper, or a change of scene. Therefore, it's only natural that the child learns to link emotional and physical need with eating. If food is used to placate needs other than hunger, a child may be conditioned to want food even when not hungry.

Another aspect of the psychological theory focuses on the role of tension and frustration in overeating. Stress situations (death of a parent, loss of a job, etc.) can cause you to eat nervously if you were so conditioned in childhood, and also to refrain from physical activity. In fact, you may want to sleep more, or you may become depressed and just want to sit.

The most interesting aspect of the psychological theory is the observation that obese and overweight people tend to become less active. This compounds the problem. Situations that cause overeating also lead to decreased physical activity and that a person who experiences periods of intense depression may also undergo a significant change in carbohydrate metabolism.

Obesity and overweight contribute to inactivity, and inactivity begets weight gain. It is indeed a vicious circle: stress, anxiety, and tension lead to compulsive eating, which shows up as fat (obesity and overweight), which leads to physical inactivity, and therefore greater stress, anxiety, and tension. Physical activity is the simplest means of breaking the vicious cycle.

The appestat and psychological theories are both valid. In many instances, obesity and overweight result from a combination of causes. What you must remember is that physical activity is the most reliable way to control weight. Also, when people exercise regularly, they don't look as flabby as most dieters. They like what they see in the mirror. Muscles are taut. Breasts do not sag. Abdomens are flat—almost washboardlike. The body is attractive and desirable.

If you are obese or very much overweight, your goal in walking should be to walk as far as you can. Don't worry about speed; distance is far more important. There are two reasons for this.

At rest, most of our energy comes from carbohydrates stored in the body. In short bursts of effort such as sprinting, practically all our energy comes from glycogen. During such exercises as walking a half hour or so, jogging, or swimming, about 50 percent of our energy comes from glycogen and 50 percent from the fat. If you exercise for an hour, there will be a significant increase in the amount of fat used. And if you exercise even longer than that, fat will supply almost 90 percent of the needed energy. So the longer you go, the more fat you burn.

Physics tells us that it takes just as much energy to move an object slowly as it does to move it quickly. Your body doesn't violate that principle. If you compare walking with jogging at moderate speeds, you will find very little difference between them in terms of energy requirements. In one mile of jogging, the average American will burn about 100 calories; in one mile of walking, he'll burn about 90 to 95 calories. If you run a mile in 10 minutes, you will burn about 10 calories per minute; if you walk a mile in 20 minutes, you will burn about five calories per minute.

If you are obese, you still can exercise, provided you do it sensibly, and under your doctor's supervision. Don't walk at an unrealistic pace. You'll become exhausted and discouraged. Use distance (or time) and go at a pace you can cope with. Your goal should be to work at your target heart rate for a minimum of 30 minutes. When this amount of walking no longer allows you to reach your target heart rate, you can gradually increase to 60 minutes or more of walking a day.

HEART ATTACK VICTIMS

Heart disease sufferers can benefit from walking. Several years ago UCLA conducted a study of 50 people with angina (chest pain). The patients were urged to walk farther and farther each day. At first, 100 feet three times a day was the limit. As their conditioning improved, some eventually walked two miles. A full 75 percent of the patients improved. Five patients said that their angina disappeared. Tests showed that where the arteries had been closed off, the heart, by expanding small arteries, had built new "bridges" of circulation around them.

What is exciting about the study is that these are not isolated examples. Some people have run marathons after suffering heart attacks. They didn't start by running; they started by walking. Doctors now know that something happens to heart disease sufferers who exercise. Aerobic exercise increases the cells of your body. New vessels may appear as if from nowhere. The reason for this is not yet clear; it may be because of the vigorous circulation of blood, or it may be due to some chemical trigger. Whatever the cause, the result is that when you get your heart rate up during the aerobic exercise, the cells throughout your body get a better cleansing and receive more life-sustaining oxygen than they did before.

Again, our emphasis is on the practical. Use your doctor's guidelines as limits; that is, how fast and how far. Don't push yourself to the point of pain or extreme discomfort. If you're excessively tired, or you don't feel right, ease up.

ARTHRITIS

If you have arthritis, you can walk safely, but like those who are obese and victims of heart disease, you must proceed cautiously. Some people have had arthritis so severe that during the initial stages of their walking program they walked in a pool, because, with the water to keep them buoyant, they weighed less and their joints were subjected to less stress. These were extreme cases, but they illustrate an important principle: don't walk during acute phases of the disease. When the pain is intense, rest.

In January 1978, the 28-year-old director of Human Services at a small community college weighed 213 pounds and had 30 percent body fat. This young man was also plagued with arthritic knees. He decided to join a walking class. At first he exercised only 20 minutes at a time. Gradually he increased until he was doing three times that much. His weight started to tumble (with help from his diet). Today he weighs 160 pounds, less than he did when he was in the eighth grade. He is convinced that walking has helped his arthritic knees. Though he still has pain every day, it is less severe because his knees are carrying less weight. His leg muscles have become stronger to compensate for his knees. Remember to consult your physician for advice about your own walking program.

EMPHYSEMA

According to the United States Public Health Service, 14 million Americans are afflicted with chronic obstructive respiratory disease. By far the most common of these ailments is emphysema. It ranks second only to heart disease as a crippler of men in their most productive years. It causes more invalidism among males than strokes, tuberculosis, and mental disorders combined. But walking can help. It is a good exercise, and possibly the best therapy, for the emphysema sufferer.

Emphysema causes an increase in the size of the alveoli (air cells) in the lungs and the destruction of capillaries. Total lung volume is increased, but the victim's actual breathing capacity is diminished. The progression of the disease is insidious. Sometimes it begins with occasional spells of coughing, and a buildup of phlegm. Unfortunately, this deceptive beginning allows the condition to progress to a more critical stage.

Both absence of activity and overexertion are dangerous for someone with emphysema. A lack of activity will make a person greatly dependent upon others, while overexertion will make breathing very difficult and frightening. As a result, the emphysema sufferer is afraid to do almost anything. He's afraid to move. Every physical effort makes him feel exhausted. So he does less and less. And the less he does, the worse he feels.

Walking is perhaps the simplest of all exercises for the emphysema patient, but it can be frightening at first. At the beginning of a program, a person's hands may turn blue when he walks. It takes a lot of courage to continue.

Yet research shows that if you start slowly, you will be able to make dramatic improvements. Although the walking will not restore lung function, it will improve the circulatory system's capacity. This means that the emphysema patient will be able to do more work. A study from about 10 years ago persuaded 11 men suffering from emphysema to exercise. The men were to do easy exercises such as arm circling and trunk twisting for 15 minutes. That was followed by a slow walk. Some men walked a full mile; others walked only half that distance. The program was keyed individually to the capabilities of each participant. Climbing stairs or bench stepping was also involved in the regimen. That was their daily exercise program.

But it did not stop there. Each man was urged to integrate physical activity into every aspect of his life. They were told to walk to the corner store instead of driving, and to take the stairs instead of the elevators if going to a building's second floor.

There were no miracles. But at the end of two months, nine of the 11 men said that they were able to go through their daily schedules with less difficulty than before. Even the exercising was less tiring than it had been at the start of the program.

The results were far more rewarding than had been expected. The researchers had expected the men to develop the psychological ability to tolerate more difficulty in breathing when walking. Predictably, that happened. But to the researchers' surprise, they noticed that actual physiological changes also occurred. Maximum exercise levels and duration increased measurably. So did the amount of oxygen the men were able to make use of each minute. There were indications that more oxygen was reaching the blood and that the suffocation associated with emphysema was lessening. The researchers speculated that the physiological changes occurred because of new blood vessels in the lungs.

Similar results were obtained with a test group in San Diego. This study noted that although no significant changes with regard to breathing function could be produced, the test subjects were able to tolerate greater amounts of exercise (due to better circulation) and that they felt better than before. They felt they could accomplish a great deal more work and they felt less dependent on others.

Because of all this, physicians are recommending exercise as a means of helping emphysema patients. It's not always easy, however. The emphysema patient often feels poorly. But if he can begin walking gradually even if it's only a few feet, he will soon find that by gradually increasing the distance he will be able to comfortably walk for five, 10, 15, and possibly even 30 minutes.

You won't change the condition of the disease. The damage is done, because of excessive smoking and/or living in a polluted environment. But you can expect your circulation to improve. As the circulation improves, you will be able to accomplish more than you'd imagined you could.

You and the Weather

Some days, the weather is going to be ideal for walking: very light breeze, temperature around 60 degrees, no clouds in sight. But what do you do when the snow starts to fall, a gale threatens to blow you off the path, or the heat makes you feel as though your shoes will melt? It may not sound very appealing to you now, but you can walk in all but the very worst weather conditions. If you succeed in making your walking program as much a part of your day as eating or sleeping, you'll probably find yourself walking through rain, snow, and sleet—and enjoying every minute of it.

Temperature extremes can be more than uncomfortable; they can be dangerous if you do not prepare yourself adequately.

Cold weather shouldn't present any serious problems if you are in reasonably good condition. It is just a matter of attitude. If you have heart problems, however, ask your doctor if it is all right for you to brave very cold weather—even if he has already given you permission to walk. High wind-chill factors are the greatest threat in cold weather, since you can get frostbite if you are inadequately protected from the wind. When you walk, your own motion against the wind increases the wind-chill factor and the risk of frostbite. Be sure that all normally exposed areas of your skin—head, face, ears, and hands—are covered. If you are wearing proper clothing, only the bitterest cold should bother you.

When it is hot, be especially careful. Cut down on your usual program. In some instances you may simply have to stop. When the thermometer hits 90 degrees, be cautious. You are going to have to experiment. But as a rule of thumb, if you are just starting to walk, have heart problems, are overweight, or more than 40 years old, set 85 degrees as your limit.

The real problem with hot weather is humidity. When your body starts to heat up, your body's cooling system is automatically turned on and you begin to sweat. The function of sweating is to keep your body cool. As your blood circulates through you, it heats up at the center part of your body. When the blood comes near the surface of the skin, the sweating and the evaporation of sweat allow the blood to cool. Consequently, your blood temperature drops a bit and the cool blood is circulated back to the center of the body. At the center, the blood heats up again and goes back to the skin. This is how your body maintains the proper temperature in a hot environment. But when the humidity is high, your thermostat doesn't work properly. The sweat doesn't evaporate, and your body temperature continues to rise.

If you continue walking vigorously while sweating profusely, you may run out of water. When this supply of body water is gone, your blood circulation is reduced and your blood pressure falls. The result can be heat exhaustion. Weakness, fainting, and shock may occur. You can avoid heat exhaustion by drinking water before, during, and after the walk. But if you don't drink water, your body temperature will continue to rise and you can get heat stroke. A person who gets heat stroke must be treated immediately. The victim must be placed in a tub of cold water or in a cold shower. If the person's temperature reaches 108 degrees, he will die.

You can avoid heat stroke and heat exhaustion or dehydration by drinking plenty of fluids, wearing light clothing, and, if it is too hot and humid, by backing off. Follow this rule: Drink a full glass of water before you begin, and more during your walk, especially if it lasts more than 30 minutes. You might also try wearing a fishnet vest (or a meshlike fabric) which will help by creating an insulating layer next to your body and thus reducing the temperature.

The only protection between you and the elements when walking is your clothing. A little bit of knowledge on how to select your clothing will go a long way in helping you "weather the weather."

In hot, humid weather, wear something that will let your body breathe as much as possible. Wear as little as you can. For the lower part of the body, nylon underwear is probably the most comfortable you can wear. Cotton is all right, too, but it can cause chafing, partly because it absorbs more perspiration than nylon and partly because the thicker cotton seams tend to irritate the thighs.

Cotton is the best material for the upper body in hot weather. It absorbs perpiration and lets perspiration evaporate easily as you walk. The motto in warm, humid weather is: Lighter is better.

Of course, there is no shortage of expensive fashions. Many walkers wear jogging outfits. These are available in different materials and designs. But if you go this route, don't wear a rubberized, plastic, or otherwise nonporous sweatsuit. In warm or hot weather, you don't want heat and moisture to be trapped. You want it to circulate and escape to keep your body cool. Those who imagine they are undergoing a kind of "Turkish bath" on the hoof are deluding themselves. They may perspire more than someone walking in shorts and lose more water and weight while they walk, but they will promptly regain that lost weight when they rush to the water fountain. The problem is that these clothes create a hot, humid environment and can trigger the phenomena of dehydration, heat exhaustion, and heat stroke. If you want to wear a suit, get one that is porous. It should be made of either cotton or a combination of cotton and a porous synthetic fiber. It should fit loosely without getting in your way.

Body heat is lost through the head, but it is also gained through the head. The head is the first part of the body struck by the powerful rays of the summer sun. So if you protect your head, you can help control your body temperature when you walk in the summer. For this, some walkers prefer to wear a lightweight cap, preferably one that is light colored, to reflect the sun's rays. They feel it keeps the head and the whole body cool.

All of this takes care of walking in Atlanta in July. But what about Central Park in February?

In cold weather, reverse the hot-weather strategy. You need to construct a personal heating system that uses your body as the furnace. To do that, dress in layers of clothing. This is very much like the insulation in your home: it keeps the heat in and the cold out. The layers of clothing trap warm air and hold it next to your body. The more you work, the warmer the air becomes. At the same time, these layers of warm air act as a barrier to the cold. A nylon windbreaker creates the strongest insulation.

After a little practice you will learn quickly what you will need for protection from the cold and the wind. In cold weather, it is always better to be overdressed than underdressed when you walk. That way you can take off clothes if you need to. This extra clothing usually is just a jacket and pants that can be tied around your waist.

In wet weather, leather shoes are better than nylon. That way your feet will stay drier. In very wet weather, put plastic bags over your socks. That may seem absurd, but people have walked in snow with suede shoes for over 10 hours and never had wet socks.

Wear socks when walking. Socks should be made of either cotton or wool. They absorb moisture well. Some walkers prefer cotton over wool because wool can be irritating. This is an individual matter.

Some people like to wear two pairs of socks, especially in cold weather. That's fine as long as one pair is lighter than the other. Don't select nylon as the lighter sock. Nylon socks tend to cause blisters.

There are two basic lengths: anklets that reach just above the shoe top, and socks that go halfway up the calf.

Anklets are better for summer walking since they are cool; the calf-high variety is more suited for winter walking because it offers greater protection.

On long walks, men can suffer irritation from athletic supporters, a problem which some walkers have solved with an apparently satisfactory, if unusual, substitute—women's panties. Some manufacturers of shorts have more or less followed the lead by designing "unisex" shorts, worn by men and women alike. Designed with a built-in nylon support, they will not rub, bind, or chafe. Another suggestion is : if you are bothered, don't wear any underwear at all. This may take a little time to get used to, but you may find it best for comfort. Also, a little petroleum jelly on the upper thighs can put an end to chafing.

It has been estimated that a hat or cap holds in 80 percent of the body's heat during winter. Put a cap on your head and, in effect, you've "capped" the heat's escape route. In fact, one walker has said, "If you want to keep your feet warm, wear a hat."

Wear a heavy knitted wool or Orlon ski cap, one you can pull down over your ears and face, when you walk in the winter. This design gives you flexibility. It can protect you from the cold and be conveniently rolled up to form a cap if you don't want to cover your face.

Many people feel the pull-down mask is the only way to go. When the wind is at your back, you can roll it up and expose your face to the sun's warm rays. But when you are heading into a strong wind, it's handy to pull down over your face to protect it from frostbite.

But a mask is a mixed blessing. Perspiration and condensation of the breath can freeze into ice around your mouth and nostrils—not the most pleasant winter experience. Some walkers have complained that a mask tends to congest the sinuses because it inhibits breathing. Nevertheless, for safety's sake, use a ski mask when the wind-chill factor is high.

Another type of mask is designed to filter polluted air that many people in urban areas must breathe. If you habitually find yourself walking alongside cars and trucks that spew out carbon monoxide, a mask of this type might be worth using.

Mittens, not gloves, give your hands the best protection in cold weather. Mittens don't have separate fingers, so cold air cannot circulate around each one. The fingers and the palm are crowded together, nice and warm in the same air space. Some people use tube socks as mittens because they go well up the arm. In really cold weather some walkers wear mittens with socks on top. Others wear gloves with mittens on top.

SPECIFIC PROBLEMS

Rain, snow, ice, hail, lightning, strong winds, fog and other harsh weather conditions can curtail your walking. So can high altitudes and darkness. But with a little bit of ingenuity, all of these can be overcome.

On warm days—any temperature higher than 70 degrees—rain is no problem for walkers. You may even welcome it. On days when the temperature dips below 60 degrees, a light rain jacket will give you sufficient protection. If you worry about your hair, you can either buy a special rain hat or carry an umbrella.

Some people love to walk in the snow. To cope with the snow, simply follow the directions for walking in the cold. Your pace will be slower, but that's okay. If the snow is deep, you'll be working just as hard as you would be at a faster pace on a clean street. If you doubt it, check your pulse.

Walking on the ice can be treacherous. It is easy to slip and injure yourself. If there is ice on the road or sidewalk, it is best to wait until later in the day when cars and people have chewed it up or the sun has melted it . If you can't do that, try to find a clean path. If that is impossible, you may walk inside on that day.

Hail can be a problem. If the hail's large, take shelter immediately. If it's small, be your own judge. Most of the time it won't harm you.

At the first sight of any lightning, head for cover. A car or building is best. If you are caught where you can't get to such cover, stay away from water, metal objects, and single trees. The best bet is to get into a hollow or a ditch. Or you might even try hiding under a small bush. Don't take chances. Get down on your knees and bend over as far as possible . . . and pray. Lightning can be deadly.

If you walk in a strong wind, you will be using up more oxygen than you would under ordinary conditions. So, if you're walking into a stiff breeze, you may want to slow down. It's like walking through deep snow. You'll get the same benefits that you would in a faster walk under normal conditions. When you set out to walk on a windy day, start walking into the wind. Then toward the end, when you are perspiring and tired, you'll have the wind to your back. It will not only make your walk easier, but it will help reduce the possibility of getting chilled.

High altitudes are a source of special problems. At 5,000 feet above sea level and higher, there is significantly less oxygen than there is at lower levels, so there is less for your body to absorb. As a result, your heart has to work hard. For every 2,500 feet that you go up, plan on taking at least a week to adjust. One way that you might adjust is to cut your program by 50 percent at the beginning. If you find yourself short of breath even at that rate, slow down even more.

When walking at night, follow these basic guidelines:

1. Face the traffic as you walk, and stay close to the edge of the road. If a car seems to be bearing down on you, step off the road and stop walking.

2. Wear light-colored clothes. White is best. If you want, wear some reflective type of tape, too.

3. Carry a flashlight so that you can see where you are walking and so you can also alert motorists.

4. Know the road you are walking on. That way you'll know where the curves and ditches are.

5. Don't look directly at the headlights of oncoming cars. They tend to blind you, and as a result you can't see where you are going. Look off to the side. You'll still be able to see the car.

Walking in the the fog is similar to walking in darkness. Follow all the guidelines for walking in darkness with one exception. Don't wear white, light-colored clothes, especially gray. Bright red or orange clothing is best.

STAYING INSIDE

Walking indoors is a solution to the problems of bad weather conditions. It has drawbacks. There are no bumps, potholes, or cars to worry about; yet walking indoors, going around and around the same track, can be boring. If you are trying to walk a mile, it may take you 20 or more laps to make it. Your mind tends to grow numb, and it is easy to become discouraged.

If you are going to walk on an indoor track for several days or more, it is best to switch direction every other day. By walking counterclockwise one day and clockwise the next, you will help avoid orthopedic problems that can result from walking on a surface that slopes to the left or right.

You can also use an indoor treadmill. A treadmill is nothing more than a conveyer belt for walking. There are two kinds—motorized and nonmotorized.

Walking on a motorized treadmill is as close to real walking as you can get without actually hitting the street. You simulate the walk almost exactly. Many motorized treadmills can be raised at one end to imitate walking uphill, making the exercise more difficult and increasing its value. Most motorized treadmills cost over $1,000.

Nonmotorized treadmills are comparatively inexpensive. They range in price from $150 to $600. They are driven by your own muscle power. They can be uncomfortable and difficult to work for long periods—15 minutes or more. The belt is on rollers, and after a period of walking, people seem to experience a "hot foot" because of the friction. Another problem is that the incline of the treadmill—5 to 10 percent—seems to aggravate leg pain in certain people. The nonmotorized treadmill is fine for slow walking for brief periods of time, but it seems to lead to foot and leg irritation at a fast pace.

Coping with Pain

We've said repeatedly that a well-designed walking program should enable you to enjoy all the benefits of the "training effect" without pain. However, no matter how carefully you follow your walking program, you probably will experience a few little aches and pains—simply because you'll be asking your body to do things that it might not have done for years.

We have included this chapter on coping with pain because we don't want a few minor physical discomforts to discourage you from walking. Here we'll explain the types of pain you may encounter and tell you how to alleviate them. As you continue to walk, you will undoubtedly gather your own little private collection of twinges and throbs—"body noises" that will be completely new to you. You are the best judge of what they mean, so pay attention to them. Most of the time your pain will be caused by improper walking technique, poor walking surfaces or shoes, and too much walking too soon.

Often the solution is so simple that you miss it. For example, several members of a walking class complained of continual pain in their left knees. Nothing seemed to help—shoes, physicians, taping. Some of the people had been walking on a banked track; others on the banked edge of the road. Suddenly, their instructor asked them to change directions frequently. That way the same leg would not always be on the down side of the bank. It worked like magic. Their pain disappeared almost immediately. The slant of the road and the bank of the track had gradually created an imbalance in their walking style and a strain on their left knees. It isn't always this simple, but this case shows how many times the solution can be found by a little self-analysis and imagination. Everyone will go through pain, more or less. That's one reason why you'll want to ask other walkers what they have experienced. Most of the solutions are just plain common sense.

The ironic thing about walking is that those organs we mainly want to exercise, the heart and lungs, are not the chief source of most of our pain. Instead it's our feet, ankles, legs, and other bones and muscles, which have to work so hard to exercise the heart and lungs, that cause the most trouble.

If you want to minimize the amount of pain, you should do three things: (1) take good care of your feet; (2) strengthen the muscles, ligaments, tendons, and joints of the feet, legs, and abdomen; and (3) develop flexibility in the body's muscular system.

Conditioning of your muscles, ligaments, joints and tendons is a process that will take place naturally and automatically as you walk. But you can help it along by supplementing your walking with calisthenics or other exercises that will develop strength and flexibility. These calisthenics do not benefit the heart and lungs, but they help the body gain more from aerobic exercise. If your muscles and joints are conditioned to work under great stress with a minimum of pain, you are ahead of the game. If not, exercise will give you the conditioning you need.

If you set up a regular exercise program for yourself to parallel your walking program, be sure it is broad and thorough enough to condition all parts of your body. The legs, ankles, and feet are more directly involved in walking than anything else. But you don't want to shortchange the upper part of your body.

FROM THE GROUND UP

The following is a summary of the types of aches and pains walkers sometimes feel. We'll begin at the bottom, discussing minor ailments of the feet, then move on up until we reach the chest, where pains can be especially troubling.

The toes. Most pain felt in the toes results from poorly fitted walking shoes. When you try on a new pair of walking shoes, be sure they fit well in the toe. Shoe widths are measured across the widest part of the foot sole, and sometimes tend to taper too drastically in the toe area. Other brands may be too wide there for your particular foot. Make sure the fit is right for you. The size of a walking shoe doesn't really tell you whether it will fit your foot. The shape of your foot finally determines the shoe you should choose for maximum comfort. Select a design that matches your foot as closely as possible.

Few things are more aggravating to a walker than toenails that cut into the flesh of the toes every time the foot comes down against the ground. The solution is simple: keep your toenails trimmed, especially at the corners.

In the foot's longest bones, the metatarsals, the stress of walking can produce fractures so small they may not be visible on an x-ray. Normally they will not have to be splinted or put into a cast. They simply heal by themselves. But it takes time, maybe a month or two, even if you do not subject them to severe strain. This doesn't mean you have to interrupt your walking program while they heal. But during this time it would be wise to walk on very soft surfaces at a reduced pace and for shorter distances.

Morton's Foot. This is not a disease, but a matter of bone structure. Normally the big toe is the longest. People who have Morton's Foot, however, have big toes that are unusually short, and the second toe is longer than the first. This condition upsets normal balance, and the weight stress falls toward the inside arch. Although many people who have Morton's Foot do not experience specific problems, others develop calluses and strains on the foot and leg.

Usually this can be corrected by wearing a special shoe insert called an orthodic, and shoes with roomy toe areas that permit the foot to slide forward without putting pressure on the ends of the toes. If you have foot pain and Morton's Foot, see a podiatrist.

Blisters. These are common ailments. Regardless of the type of shoe worn and the protective measures taken, foot blisters continue to be a problem for many people. They become a major problem only when they are severe enough to affect the quantity and quality of walking. Problems also occur when infection develops.

Foot blisters are caused by heat. They are really burns produced by friction. The best way to prevent blisters is to prevent the friction that causes them. Here are some recommendations.

1. Buy high-quality shoes and make sure they fit properly.

2. Take good care of your shoes. Don't allow them to get brittle so that "hot spots" develop.

3. Break in new shoes before walking very far. A good idea is to first wear the shoes around the house for a few minutes each day. As they begin to soften, wear them for walking short distances (10 to 20 minutes). As they start to break in, you can wear them for longer distances.

4. Wear socks to help prevent blisters. The socks should be clean and fit snugly.

When a blister does develop, prevent infection by keeping the area clean. Do not puncture small blisters immediately. If you do puncture a blister once it has grown larger, puncture it with a sterile needle to release the fluid, squeezing gently with sterile gauze. Do not remove the skin. Place a pad of gauze and, possibly, foam rubber over the open blister. Continue to walk if you can do so without significant pain. Consult your physician or podiatrist at the first sign of infection or complications.

Walker's heel. This is a term some people use to describe a group of heel problems that include bone bruises and heel spurs (painful bony growths on the heel bone itself). These ailments are normally caused by walking on a hard surface, stepping on sharp objects with force enough to cause a bruise, or wearing poorly designed walking shoes. These complaints don't lend themselves to a quick cure. Rest is good for them, but not always desirable for the person who wants to maintain his or her conditioning.

As far as treatment is concerned, the best thing is a heel "donut." This is nothing more than a foam pad with a hole cut in it. You can place the foam pad over the bone spur with the sensitive spot protruding through the hole. Then tape the donut to your foot. Many people have had excellent success with this. If this doesn't work for you, see a podiatrist.

Achilles tendon injuries. The Achilles tendon is the thick tendon at the back of the leg that connects the heel and foot to the back of the calf muscle. It controls the hinge-like action of the ankle with every walking step and therefore does a lot of work during a walk. Achilles tendon injuries are extremely debilitating. Some people have said, in fact, that once you have an Achilles problem, you will always have a problem.

Sports medicine experts have identified three types of problems with the Achilles tendon. The first is tendinitis, which is an inflammation of the tendon. The second is a partial rupture, which is a tearing of the tendon fibers. The third is a complete rupture, or a complete break, of the tendon itself. The last two are not common to most walkers.

Tendinitis is usually caused by a sudden change in routine, such as different types of shoes, or walking on grass and then switching to cinders, or going from one type of training to another. Symptoms of tendinitis are pain and stiffness an hour or so following activity, slight swelling, pain on contraction and stretching of the calf muscles, and tenderness when squeezing pressure is applied at the tendon's narrowest point. Walking becomes very difficult and painful.

Tendons also become inflamed and swollen when they are constricted by equipment. If you feel pain in your Achilles tendon, your walking shoes could be the culprit.

The heels may be too low or too hard, or the backs may be too tight, straining or crowding the tendon. Perhaps the arch support in the shoes is not adequate. Tendinitis can also be caused by years of wearing heeled shoes. The heels favored by Americans shorten the Achilles tendons and make them less flexible. The very act of walking often tightens these tendons even more, just as it develops the muscles of the legs. This is one reason why stretching exercises are important to the walker. They limber up the tendons and counteract the effects of walking and the wearing of heels.

Self-treatment of tendinitis can be summarized in a few sentences. If it hurts you, put cold water or ice on the injured area. Reduce your activity until what pain there is isn't intolerable. Slow down or stop if pain gets worse while exercising. In simple terms, if you're not hurting, you probably aren't hurting yourself.

When you first injure your Achilles tendon, stretching should be avoided at all costs. Overstretching led to the problem in the first place. Walk on flat, smooth, straight surfaces. Do not do any fast walking. As long as there is tendon inflammation and pain, ice or cold water after each walking session may be helpful. But this will not really cure the injury—it simply helps you endure the pain.

To prevent Achilles tendinitis from developing, make sure that you do plenty of stretching in your warm-ups. Suggested stretching exercises include standing on the heels of the feet, drawing the toes up as far as possible, or putting your toes on a two-inch board and stretching the heel downward. Another good idea is to walk barefooted whenever possible.

Also avoid sudden and violent changes in routine: for example, walking on a level surface and then suddenly changing to walking on hills; walking on a track and then suddenly switching to a road; or walking short distances and then suddenly walking long distances.

Shin splints. Shin splints are a pain on the front

of the shin. If you have a shin splint you will feel pain in the lower leg when you put weight on your foot. You'll probably also find that your shin is tender to the touch. When you run your fingers along the shin, you may feel a roughened area along the bone.

Although the name implies a splintering or damage to the shin bone, it may be any of several conditions. Here are a few possibilities: (1) You may have a muscle imbalance caused by a "toeing out" of the feet or other improper body mechanics; (2) there may be a hairline fracture of one of the bones in the lower leg; (3) a muscle spasm may occur because of the swelling of the muscle in the front of the leg; (4) the tendon that is attached to the bone of the lower leg may be inflamed; (5) the same tendon or the muscle may be torn from the bone; (6) the membrane between the two bones of the lower leg may be irritated; (7) your arch may drop somewhat, thereby irritating one or more of the tendons of the lower leg.

You can prevent shin splints by taking care when choosing your footwear and the surfaces you walk on. A good pair of shoes with a rippled sole and heel is probably best. Shoes with cushioned soles are a must. It's also a good idea to have a shoe with a low heel. If possible, switch from a hard to a soft walking surface. A golf course or a local park offers the walker a chance to work out on grass, which is much softer than pavement or a track. If you walk on a track, vary the direction of your walking. Instead of always going counterclockwise, walk clockwise on alternate days so that you do not always place stress on the inside of the same leg as you go around the turns.

Also try to avoid walking on your toes. This has been cited as one of the causes of shin splints. Put a sponge heel pad in the heel section of your shoe to help absorb some of the stress from walking on harder surfaces. You can also try placing a molded crest under the toes.

To prevent shin splints from occurring, it's also a good idea to condition the muscles in the front of the leg.

Walking does a great deal to strengthen the muscles in the back of the leg. And as a result, muscle imbalance occurs. The muscles in the back of the leg become a lot stronger than the ones in the front, and this sets you up for shin splints. To compensate, you'll want to strengthen the muscles in the front. Doing foot flexors with weights or isometric exercises can help. Flex your foot up and down against resistance. If you don't have weights handy to strap on your feet, sit with your legs dangling, feet not touching the floor, and have a friend hold your feet while you try to pull your toes up. Do this for three sets of 10 each day.

The knee. The knee, the largest and most complicated joint of the body, is a true hinge joint. The two main bones of the joint are the thigh and shin bone. All leg muscles and ligaments, which are essential to the efficient movement and support of the joint, are attached to the thigh and shin bones.

Although the knee is the largest joint in the body, it is vulnerable to injuries, largely because of a poor bone arrangement. Its main support of the joint is from tendons and ligaments, and it has very little defense against a blow from the side. Injuries to the knee joint can be disabling. In some instances, they can keep you from participating in athletics, especially contact sports.

But, despite its vulnerability, your knee can stand a remarkable degree of stress and still work well. It is able to survive even a brutal crush by several 250-pound football players hitting it from different angles—strains beyond the imagination of most people.

On your walk through the neighborhood or along the beach, your knees are not completely safe from stress. Usually knee pains are associated with the kneecap— beneath it or along its sides. Sometimes the kneecap does not move smoothly against the lower end of the thighbone as it should, and the knee becomes increasingly irritated and swollen as you walk. If you have this problem, you may have to limit your walking. But first experiment with different walking methods. Many doctors think this problem may be caused or aggravated by the way your foot strikes the ground. If you walk indoors on a banked track in one direction for long distances, say 20 to 25 laps, your knees may be headed for trouble. Even a subtle slope such as that on a banked road or on a beach may also cause problems.

Many walkers and runners develop a painful affliction called runner's knee in which the kneecap moves from side to side with each step. The reason is most often a foot that collapses when walking. When the foot collapses, the lower leg rotates inward and the kneecap moves to the inside. Repeated foot strikes and a poor foot structure will adversely affect the knee. Treatment usually consists of orthodics to control foot function. It's also important that the participant do leg exercises to strengthen and stretch the muscles on the front of the thighs.

Muscle cramps and spasms. When one of your muscles contracts powerfully and painfully, you have a muscle cramp. The contraction may occur at any time—at rest as well as during activity. Cramps usually occur without warning. Occasionally, however, you may be able to feel one building up.

Among the causes of muscle cramps are fatigue; cold; imbalance of salt, potassium, and water levels; a sharp blow; and overstretching of unconditioned muscles. (The cramps that a person gets when stretching in bed are brought on by a combination of fatigue and overstretching of unconditioned muscles.)

You can probably reduce the chances of muscle cramps by maintaining a proper diet, making sure you warm up properly prior to vigorous activity, and stopping activity before you become extremely fatigued. Tapering off is a good idea.

Once a cramp does occur, it can usually be stopped by stretching the muscle affected and firmly kneading it. Usually, a sense of tightness or dull pain will follow, making it necessary to apply heat and massage to the area to restore circulation. If you're plagued with frequent cramps, drinking adequate fluid and eating foods high in salt and potassium, along with muscle strengthening and stretching exercises, will usually eliminate the problem.

Sprains and strains. Cramps and spasms are essentially painful contractions of muscle tissue. A strain is a stretching or tearing of a muscle or tendon; a sprain is a stretching or tearing of a ligament. Small blood vessels in the area break and pain develops when the surrounding tissue swells up and overstimulates sensitive nerve endings.

Two common problems are ankle strains and sprains. Obviously, you should watch where you're going. This means that even if you are the casual type and not too finicky about walking on a particular kind of surface, you should at least learn how to pick your way among the potholes and skillfully sidestep any beer cans in your path. If you aren't very good at that and manage to sprain or strain your ankle, you'll have to suspend your walking program until it is healed.

Muscle soreness and stiffness. Even people who have been walking for years complain of regular soreness and stiffness. The pain may occur immediately following the activity or after some delay, usually 24 to 48 hours. Often the discomfort lasts for only a few days, although after periods of severe exercise, it may last for a week. The most commonly affected muscles are the calves and front and back muscles of the thigh.

Medical authorities aren't certain what causes soreness and stiffness. The pain during and immediately following exercise is probably due to waste products formed during exercise and left in the fluid that surrounds the cells. When stiffness occurs approximately 24 to 48 hours after exercise, it may be the result of small muscle tears or localized contractions of muscles.

It is practically impossible to completely avoid muscle soreness and stiffness. But you can reduce the intensity of the pain by planning your conditioning program so that you progress gradually, especially during the early stages. That approach will allow the muscles of the body to adapt themselves to the stress placed upon them. If you become sore and stiff from physical activity, doing some additional light exercises or general activity will often provide temporary relief, though the pain usually returns when you stop. Tapering off will also help to avoid such undesirable after effects. Massage will, too.

Back pains. Don't fool around when you get back pains, especially if they are in the lower back. The low back pain can signal a slipped spinal disc. Obviously, back problems cannot be diagnosed on the walking path, but if you have a slipped disc, you'll know it—fast.

Some lower back pains result from exercising after years of relative inactivity. You will have to guess at the seriousness of these pains by the way you feel at the time; that is, how intense they are, how much they cripple you, and so on. In any case, go slow. If for any reason you think further exercise might cause any harm, ask your doctor.

There are, of course, several traditional explanations for back pain. You've probably heard them already, but they're worth repeating. Improper sitting posture can lead to low back problems. As in lifting, the back should be kept erect. Sitting slouched in a chair puts unnecessary tension on the back muscles. Furniture that is constructed without regard for body structure can cause strain, fatigue, and muscle pain. Sitting for prolonged periods of time causes shortening of certain postural muscles, particularly the hamstring muscles. If you sit all day at work, you must do stretching exercises regularly to keep hamstring muscles at their proper length.

A bed that is too soft or sags in the middle is the worst enemy of any back. No matter how you lie on this kind of mattress, your muscles are under constant tension all night long. It is no wonder that these muscles, the spinal erectors being the ones most often affected, are sore in the morning. Many medical experts suggest the use of a board under the mattress to alleviate the condition.

But the real problem is poor fitness; specifically, weak abdominals. At the pelvis, the weight of the upper body is transferred to the lower limbs. The pelvis, or pelvic girdle, is balanced on the rounded heads of the thigh bones. To the pelvis are attached numerous muscles which hold it in place. Some of the muscles involved are the abdominals, hamstrings, gluteals, and hip flexors. An imbalance or weakness in those muscles can lead to pelvic misalignment, which usually cause the pelvis to tilt forward or backward.

If the abdominal muscles which are attached to the front of the pelvis and hold it up are weak, the top of the pelvis will drop and tilt forward. The sacrum (just below the spine) also tilts forward, putting increased tension on the sacroiliac joint and the ligaments located on the front of the lumbar vertebrae. Forward tilt of the pelvis leads to lordosis, or sway back. This is when the "slipped disc" injury most often occurs.

In addition to abdominal weakness, a lack of strength in the gluteals and/or hamstrings can also lead to forward pelvic tilt. While the abdominals stabilize the pelvis by pulling upward on the front, the gluteals and hamstrings contribute to stabilizing by pulling down on the rear of the pelvis.

Exercises must be done to strengthen the abdominals and gluteals. Usually the walking does it for the gluteals. But the abdominal muscles must be conditioned with more specific exercise. If in doubt, see your doctor.

Quite a few walkers have found that their back pain disappeared after walking and abdominal exercises. But this isn't a miracle cure. On the contrary, you must be extremely cautious. If you have back trouble and do not approach walking with common sense and care, you can make the condition worse.

Side stitch. Side stitch has many names. It is called a pain in the side, a stitch in the side, side ache, or just plain stitch. Sometimes it frightens people because it occurs near the chest area. There are as many explanations of the cause of side stitch as there are names to describe it. But there are probably two basic causes.

The first is improper breathing. This causes spasms in the diaphragm. To reduce the problem, "belly breathing" is suggested. That is, when you inhale, the diaphragm should distend, pushing the abdominal wall out. When you exhale, the diaphragm should be pushed in so that the belly is flattened. It's just the reverse of what you normally do.

The second cause is probably the more common. It's a spasm of the ligaments that are connected to the liver, pancreas, stomach, and intestines. These ligaments are put under stress when you walk vigorously. The bouncing action causes these ligaments to stretch, thereby causing pain. You may be able to end side stitch by simply gripping your side and pushing it in. In severe cases, you can lie on your back and raise your feet in the air or even try standing on your head or hands.

There are some other things you can try. Don't eat or drink within three hours before walking; during the attack bend forward, inhale deeply, and push the belly out; if the pain is intolerable, lie flat on your back, raise your legs over your head, and support your hips.

CHEST PAIN: HOW SERIOUS IS IT?

Any pain in the chest, no matter what its cause, can be troubling—especially if you've reached middle age. Such pain often results in unnecessary concern, because it can be caused by factors that are in no way related to the condition of your heart. However, chest pain should never be ignored or allowed to persist.

Here we'll explain the causes of chest pain—everything from heartburn to heart attacks. We hope this will be able to put your mind at ease about some kinds of chest pain, while inducing you to remain extremely cautious about other kinds.

We are warned so much about heart disease that the slightest twinge in the chest area can conjure up frightening visions of permanent disability, or even death, from cardiovascular disturbances. A seizure in the chest can be, and often is, caused by a cardiovascular disease. But far more often it is caused by a simpler and less damaging ailment, such as heartburn or a strained muscle. Or it can be psychosomatic.

Psychosomatic chest pain. An estimated 20 million people in the United States are cardiac patients without heart disease. These people suffer symptoms that are common to heart disease, such as palpitations, shortness of breath, exhaustion, and chest pain; but the symptoms are really only reactions to stress.

Mind and body are so inseparable that every emotional experience we have is also a physical event. By simply thinking about a problem, you can raise your pulse, cause sweating, bring on headaches, and any number of other symptoms. In effect, this is self-inflicted stress, and that stress can cause pain.

Researchers have recently discovered that certain events, such as a change of job or a visit of a relative, can bring on illness—even the common cold. After the events are resolved—the relative returns home, the new job works out well—the ailments clear up. But often, simply talking about the situations after the fact is sufficient to cause the physical symptoms to recur. For some people, just *thinking* about a bad heart is enough to give them physical symptoms.

It is very difficult to distinguish psychosomatic heart pain from actual pain. Psychosomatic pain usually is vague. The person "feels" like he has a chest pain, but he can't be specific. Usually the tests given by the doctor also reveal no heart damage or disease.

Muscular causes. The pain experienced by a psychosomatic patient may originally be caused by a muscle spasm. A pulled pectoral (chest muscle) or a strained intercostal (side muscle) can cause a great deal of pain. A pulled muscle produces pain which is felt near the surface, and movements such as swinging the arm across the chest can initiate or worsen the pain. Bruised muscles and ligaments may cause pain during deep breathing, and they normally remain sensitive to touch. Pressure during sleep from a hand, mattress button, or even a wrinkled sheet may aggravate bruised muscles. Pain associated with this kind of condition usually occurs only during a certain motion and when pressure is applied to the area. Rest and time are usually the best treatments.

Heartburn. The pain brought on by indigestion, or heartburn, is frequently confused with heart pain. But it has nothing to do with the heart. Acid from the stomach backs up into the esophageal tube, causing contractions of the circular muscle of the esophagus. Milk or plain water may give temporary relief, but a simple diet of less highly seasoned food is the best prevention. Heartburn is often confused with real heart disease. If you can attribute the pain to a specific food, your worries are over. If you can't, see your doctor.

Angina pectoris. Known as the "cardiac pain of effort," angina pectoris usually develops during exercise, when emotion is high, or after a heavy meal. It is the result of a temporary failure of the coronary arteries to supply enough oxygenated blood to the heart muscle. Such a failure is usually caused by obstructions to coronary circulation.

Almost anyone can experience angina: people who have recovered from a heart attack, people who are going to have an attack, and some people who will never have an attack. The problem is that your heart muscle is simply not getting enough blood and oxygen. See your doctor if you suspect its presence. In all probability he will permit you to walk as long as you can walk without pain. Don't push yourself to exhaustion. Your doctor will probably want you to be very specific about where the pain appears when you're walking (if it does) so he can fully understand your condition.

Angina pain is usually not sharp; it usually is heavy, giving the victim the sensation that he or she is being squeezed or crushed in the center of the chest. The discomfort often spreads to the left shoulder, arm, or hand, where it may be felt as numbness. Pains may occur days, weeks, months, even years apart. The best treatment following an attack is to rest and to avoid excitement and fatigue.

The pains associated with coronary heart disease are varied, yet similar to angina. They may be sharp or mild with a feeling of numbness. A good rule to follow regarding chest pain is that if the pain abruptly ends after exertion, see your physician.

If you experience any of these pains, particularly the kind that cause heavy pressure and radiate up the neck or down the arm, see your doctor. A very heavy pressure, as if someone were sitting on top of your chest; an extreme tightness, like a clenched fist inside the center of your chest; a feeling something like indigestion, a stuffiness high in your stomach or low in your throat, may signal a heart attack. Whenever you have a strong symptom that resembles any one of these, stop walking and get to your doctor.

You may have gone through a stress ECG before you started a walking program and passed it with flying colors. If so, your chances of having this experience are relatively small. But don't become cocky. A stress ECG, like most tests doctors perform on you, is not 100 percent reliable.

In the final analysis, your body, not somebody else's electronic equipment, has the last word. Listen to it.

Staying with It

You're convinced, right? We've succeeded in talking you into beginning a walking program and getting yourself into shape. That's great.

However, if you're like many sedentary people who know they ought to be more active, you may already be wondering how long you'll be able to stay with your program of physical conditioning. You may doubt your own stick-to-itiveness. Maybe you're asking yourself: "How long will it be before I lose interest, or develop a blister and give up, or invent any number of other silly excuses for not walking?"

Don't let these worries keep you from starting to walk. Begin now, and refer to this chapter whenever you feel a need for another dose of encouragement. We're now going to tell you exactly how to stay with it.

THE PROPER ATTITUDE

Step One: Set a goal. You're not going to get far without a specific objective. Goals are important in life. They give you something specific to work toward and a way to measure your progress. When you're setting a goal, avoid vague generalizations: "I want to get into shape," or "I want to lose weight." Instead, set precise long-term, intermediate, and short-term goals.

For example, if you want to lose weight, find out what your best weight is and decide how much weight you want to lose in six months or a year. If you want to lose 20 pounds during that period, that is your long-term goal. Your short-term goal might be three pounds by the end of the first month. (Your intermediate goal would be somewhere in between.) Your long-term goal might be 90 minutes of walking a day afer 20 weeks. A short-term goal may be 20 minutes of walking a day. An intermediate goal, on the other hand, may be to add one minute of walking a day over the next month.

What kind or how many goals should you set? Take stock of yourself right now. What would you like to do? Whatever it is, write it down now. Even if it seems unrealistic at this time, put it on a sheet of paper or card and save it. These are your long-term goals. Once a week, take out the sheet of paper and look at it. Write down your progress and what seems to be preventing you from achieving everything you want though walking.

Next, you need to plan how you are going to reach those goals. Write it down, and be specific. For example, how many minutes of walking are you going to increase each week to get to your long-term goal? Jot down some motivators you are going to use to help yourself walk.

Finally, make a note of what you'll do today; not tomorrow, but today. Write down how long, at what time, and where you're going to walk. Each morning, as soon as you get up, do the same thing until you reach your long-term goal.

Step Two: Record your progress. For some of us, the thing that makes football, basketball, or ice hockey interesting is the competition. If competition really gets you moving, you can get it from walking. Just use a progress chart. A progress chart lets you compete with yourself. It also tells you and anyone else who looks at it how well you're doing and how close you're getting to your goal. It gives you a feeling of accomplishment.

The chart doesn't have to be complicated. The simplest one is a calendar with the information written in.

Many people record their mileage on a map. Your regular walking route may take you around the same section of your neighborhood every day, but you can mark off your distance on a map as though you were walking cross-country. By the end of a year, you may find that you've walked a distance equal to that between San Francisco and San Diego or between New York and Miami. This helps in setting long-term goals, too. For instance, you can promise yourself that you'll walk from Chicago to Dallas this summer.

Step Three: Make a time commitment. Have you ever noticed how easily you slip into routines? Perhaps you always brush your teeth before, not after, your shower in the morning; always put your left, not your right, shoe on first; take the same route to work every day. And have you ever noticed how you tend to feel you've forgotten to do something important if anything should interfere with this strange little ritual? You may find it easy to stay with a walking program if you can allow it to become part of your daily routine—so much a part that you'll feel compelled to walk despite your own excuses for skipping a day. If you can get yourself into the habit of walking at a certain time every day, you'll accept it as part of your regular daily schedule and not just something to do during odd moments.

Whatever you do, don't worry about taking the time. Your co-workers may take a two-hour, three-martini lunch and think nothing of it. And they may cast a scornful eye at you as you go off to take your walk at noon. But you'll be doing something positive for your body, and it will make you feel better, more productive, and more alive.

Step Four: Choose the best time of day. The best time depends on you. Some walkers like to walk early in the morning, some even before daybreak. They seem to like the solitude available at that hour, when the streets are still empty of traffic and people. They can slowly get their minds and bodies going and do a little thinking in the silence. And if they are walking where they can see the horizon, they can savor the exhilarating sight of dawn.

If you do walk before going to work, it is probably a good idea to nibble on something beforehand so your body has the fuel it needs for the walk. There are really no iron-clad rules, but something very light such as a piece of toast and a small glass of orange juice is best.

Some people skip lunch and use the time to walk. It gets them out of the office or house and into a refreshing mid-day break. Other walkers wait until they have left their work, put their jobs behind them, and headed home. A walk at this time provides a nice transition for them, a time to work off some of the day's tensions so that they don't have to carry them into family life.

Late evening seems to appeal to some people as the best time. There is both good news and bad news about walking late in the evening. First, the bad news: when you make walking the last item on your agenda for the day, it often gets treated that way—last. You tend to put other things in place of it. You either forget it, "just don't have the time," or don't have the energy to do it. Now for the good news. When you walk late in the evening, you'll find the walk relaxing. You'll be able to unwind. Some walkers find the late evening walk the best sleeping aid ever invented.

Step Five: Dress the part. If possible, have a special outfit and wear it only for walking. Anything comfortable—an old pair of shorts or jeans and a sweatshirt, for instance—will do. How you look is not the point; it's how you feel. In changing from regular clothes into a "walking outfit," you also psych yourself up for the activity. In effect, you're telling yourself you mean business and really intend to collect your rewards.

Step Six: Think the part. What happens in your head is almost as important as what happens to your body, because if you don't enjoy what you're doing, you'll begin to find reasons for not doing it.

Before you walk, try to get yourself into a positive, active frame of mind. As you walk, be aware of what's happening to your body. Feel your muscles work. Concentrate on the rhythmic flow of your movements. Walking can be a pleasurable sensory experience if you can learn to think of it that way.

Step Seven: Walk with others. If you're married, your spouse has to be on your side. A study conducted at the Heart Disease and Stroke Control Program bears this out. Men in an exercise program did one hour of physical activity three times a week for eight months. If the wife encourged participation, the individual's attendance was good; if the wife was neutral or had negative feelings about the exercise, attendance was much poorer. The conclusion: the spouse's attitude was critical.

Walking with a friend gives you the advantage of companionship and encouragement. And you will walk more if you have someone to talk to and to keep you company. This is also a good way to assure yourself that you can pass the talk test.

In an investigation conducted at the University of Toronto, scientists reported a greater dropout rate for individual, rather than group, programs: only 47 percent of those on individual programs were still active at 28 weeks, compared with 82 percent of those in the group programs. If you feel your motivation is weak, walk with a partner or with several friends.

Step Eight: Pick a pleasing route. Where you choose to walk is up to you. The range of choices obviously is unlimited—at least as far as space is concerned.

Maybe you're lucky enough to live in a town that offers not just walking space—every town has that—but different kinds of spaces to make your walks as interesting as possible. You'll soon have your favorite, and you'll probably discover new ones every week. While making discoveries, always consider safety. Traffic must always be taken into account. And some city areas are just not safe enough to walk through at any hour. The best way to protect yourself against these possible dangers is to check over the route you plan to use ahead of time.

When you choose a route, pay close attention to the surface. A lot of walkers say grass is the very best surface for walking. City dwellers can usually find some strip of grass or other unpaved areas to walk on, even if it's only the boulevard along a street. If you can't find a nice, springy green surface to use, pavement is an alternative. One good thing about pavement—you don't have to travel far to find it. But it does have its drawbacks. Most foot and leg problems are either caused or aggravated by walking on hard surfaces like concrete or asphalt. Wearing good, shock-absorbing walking shoes can help avoid this.

If you must use the street instead of the sidewalk, you must be alert for cars. Even if you wear reflective strips on your clothing, you may not be seen by a motorist. Walk as you drive—defensively.

There's another thing you can do to have an enjoyable walk even if you're not surrounded by trees, grass, and fresh country air. Find an old residential area with beautiful homes and meandering streets that can occupy your attention while you walk. Stay away from traffic lights and congested areas where there is a lot of stop-and-go walking. They can cause you to lose momentum and break your stride because you will be concerned about collisions.

Wherever you go, be sure to watch out for dogs. Most walkers have found that the best way to get rid of dogs is to talk sternly to them. Act as if you are their master. Don't show fear. Just speak directly to them, point your finger, and shout.

There are some things to watch out for if you plan to walk in the country. Make sure you're not trespassing. Also, be careful that you don't get carried away by the beauties of nature, the music of the birds, and get lost.

Step Nine: Walk tall. Don't worry about what other people think. As you're walking down Main Street, you may think that everyone is looking at you. So what!— you're doing something good for your body; they're not. You have to learn that some of the stares people are giving you are really nothing more than envy. At least one psychologist has said that the reason he felt people stared at him as he walked was because they wished they had his ambition. People also might be looking at you with admiration.

You may also feel a little embarrassed about walking next to the road. If you do this very often, you'll find that people will ask you questions, such as, "Did your car break down? Can we give you a lift?" You have several alternatives. First, you can tell them, "No thanks, I'm walking." Second, you can tell them, "I only have a few more steps to go." Third, you can pretend you're going shopping. Finally, you can take your dog with you. Everyone knews that a dog needs exercise.

If these don't seem to work, then it may be best to walk where you can't be seen. One couple was so embarrassed about walking outside that they decided to walk in the huge underground parking garage of their apartment complex.

THE WALKING COMMUTER

Many walkers we know have managed to work their walking program into their daily commuting. They're proof of what we've been saying throughout this book: walking is the easiest of all exercises to build into your routine.

Some people who must drive or travel by public transportation for several miles to get to work each day, assume that they cannot walk to work. They can't walk the entire distance, that's true. But they *can* park their cars or get off the train a couple of miles from work and walk the rest of the way.

If you drive to work, you might even save money if you walk part of the way. As every long-distance commuter knows, the longest part of the drive to work is inevitably the last mile or two, as you near the congested area that everyone is trying to reach. If you're really unlucky, it can take the last 10 minutes of an hour-long drive to go just four blocks. If you parked your car, four, six, or eight blocks from work, you could probably walk that distance in the same amount of time it takes you to drive, fight for a parking space, and get to your office. And chances are that you'll pay less for parking because you won't be fighting for a prime parking space. Depending on the location, if you play your cards right, you may even be able to find a free space.

You can continue to walk after arriving at work. For instance, use the stairs instead of the elevator. At mid-morning, walk back and forth along the hall while everyone else is filling up on coffee and Danish. Use the stairs when you leave for lunch, and again when you return. Be sure to walk to and from the restaurant. Hit the hallway again at mid-afternoon, and ignore the elevator at day's end. Walk to your car.

If you follow such a routine faithfully, five days a week, you will burn up an extra 2,000 calories each week.

Employers could make an important contribution to their employees' welfare and productivity by encouraging them through financial and physical incentives to walk to work. Here is one idea that deserves consideration. A company could rent parking lots a mile or two away from its offices so employees could park there and walk to work. In case of bad weather, umbrellas and perhaps even other rain gear could be placed at the office and parking lots for use by walking employees. This system has the built-in potential for progress checks and awards. Some sort of sign-in or sign-out procedure could be used to check whether employees use the facility. Many companies are already awarding their physically fit employees with special financial incentives. This system would lend itself perfectly to such a program. It could also help companies that don't have facilities for exercise.

The chief financial officer of several companies will read this and think, "Terrific. But how much is all this walking going to cost and who's going to pay for it?" In a way, it would be just like any other investment. It might cost a few dollars at first, but that money would quickly pay dividends in terms of healthier, more productive employees who take fewer days off for illness. And it probably wouldn't hurt a company's insurance rates.

But if this seems too complicated, there are plenty of simple ideas, too. Here's one that wouldn't take more than an hour or two to put into practice. A company could measure the distance from some of the more common subway stations and bus stops to its central office. Suggested times and distances could be recorded. Ford Motor Company in Dearborn, Michigan, has already done this. The company has devised an activity called "The Headquarters Hustle." The Hustle is to encourage employees to exercise during the course of the working day.

To do "The Headquarters Hustle" an employee first visits the Health Services Department and picks up a map of the measured distances throughout the company area. The next step is to chart a daily walking course.

Guidelines included with the map explain that walking can produce cardiovascular fitness if the pace is sufficient and if the exercise is performed three to four times a week. In the guidelines is a starter program for those who are "out of shape."

Ford's rationale for the walking program was to let the employees know that they could indeed do something physically constructive in their working clothes and in a relatively short span of time, despite not having physical facilities for an exercise program on location.

Urban planners could also help the walker-traveler-commuter. Urbanization in America (and throughout the Western world) has paved over and plowed under much of the scenic beauty that once encouraged people to get out of their houses and walk. Billboards and fast-food restaurants are not exactly soul-stirring. Motor vehicles have taken control of our cities to such an extent that pedestrians are being shunted aside and crowded out. Cars, not the people who drive them, have become the masters of modern cities. Happily, enlightened city planners now push for improved public transportation (which would relieve the crush of automobile traffic), and for the designation of certain streets or blocks as "pedestrian traffic only." Attractive malls and parks are becoming more common in our business areas. We can only hope that this trend continues.

WALKING INTO THE FUTURE

However you choose to stay with your walking program, the important thing is to do it regularly and faithfully. The physical and mental benefits—as well as a very real sense of accomplishment—will be all yours. You may not walk around the world or the length of the Appalachian Trail (which stretches from Maine to Georgia) or even into the next town, but if you're walking at all, you'll be doing yourself a world of good. The great walkers—the people who hold records of distance or speed or endurance—demonstrate their own stamina, but they also demonstrate that there is within all of us the power to do more than we think possible. We only have to try.

References

Adams, G.M., and deVries, H.A. "Physiological Effects of an Exercise Training Regimen Upon Women Aged 52 to 79." *Journal of Gerontology* 28 (1973).

Allsen, P.E.; Harrison, J.M.; and Vance, B. *Fitness For Life.* Dubuque, Iowa: William C. Brown, 1976.

Ambrus, L. *Exercise and Emphysema.* Washington, DC: Veteran's Administration Hospital, 1965.

American Medical Association. "Exercise Stress Testing of the Apparently Healthy Individual by Allied Health Personnel." Unpublished statement, November 1974.

—————. *Guide to Prescribing Exercise Programs.* Chicago: American Medical Association, 1976.

Anderson, B. *Stretching.* Fullerton, Calif., 1975.

Andrews, V. "The Joy of Jogging." *The New York Times,* December 27, 1976/January 3, 1977.

Aronow, W.S., and Stemmer, E.A. "Two-Year Follow-Up of Angina Pectoris: Medical or Surgical Therapy." Annals of Internal Medicine, February 1975.

Asher, W.L. *Treating the Obese.* New York: Medcom Press, 1974.

Astrand, P.O., and Rodahl, K. *Textbook Work Physiology.* New York: McGraw-Hill, 1977.

Barnard, R.J. "The Heart Needs Warm-Up Time." *The Physician and Sportsmedicine,* January 1976.

Bednar, R. "A Dog-Gone Good Way To Exercise." *Fitness For Living,* September/October 1968.

Behnke, A.R., and Wilmore, J.H. *Evaluation And Regulation Of Body Build And Composition.* Englewood Cliffs, N.J.: Prentice-Hall, 1974.

Beller, A.S. *Fat and Thin.* New York, N.Y.: Farrar, Straus and Giroux, 1977.

Beloc, N.D. "The Relationship of Health Practices and Mortality." *Preventive Medicine* 2 (1973).

Benson, H. *The Relaxation Response.* New York: William Morrow, 1975.

Bingham, D. "Walk Away From Leg Pain." *Fitness For Living*, September/October 1971.

Brinkman, G. "They Do It By The Millions!" *Fitness For Living*. July/August 1969.

Brock. T. "Let's Take A Nice Brisk Walk." *Fitness For Living*. January/February 1968.

Brody, J.E. "Jogging Is Like a Drug: Watch the Dosage, Beware the Problems." *The New York Times*, November 10, 1976.

Brunner, D. "The Influence of Physical Activity on Incidence and Prognosis of Ischemic Heart Disease." In Raab, Wilhelm, (ed.), *Prevention of Ischemic Heart Disease, Principles and Practice*. Springfield, Ill.: Charles C Thomas, 1966.

Bucher, C.A. "Exercise Is 'Plain Good Business'" *Reader's Digest*, February 1976.

Cantwell, J.D. "Athletes' Hearts: Disease and Nondisease." *The Physician and Sportsmedicine*, September 1973.

Claremont, A., and Bostian, L. "Where Do You Begin?" *Runner's World*, September 1976.

Conniff, J.C.G. "Getting On A Good Footing," *The New York Times Magazine*, April 23, 1978.

Conrad, C.C. "How Different Sports Rate In Promoting Physical Fitness." *Medical Times*, May 1976.

Consumer Guide Magazine, eds. *The Running Book*, Skokie, Ill,: Publications International, 1978.

Cooper, K.H. *Aerobics*. New York: Bantam Books, 1968.

_____ . *The New Aerobics*. New York: Bantam Books, 1970.

_____ . *Aerobics For Women*. New York: Bantam Books, 1972.

_____ . *The Aerobics Way*. New York: M. Evans and Co., 1977.

Cooter, G.R. et al. "Do Long Hair and Football Uniforms Impair Heat Loss?" *The Physician and Sportsmedicine*, February 1975.

Corday, E. "Status of Coronary Bypass Surgery." *Journal of the American Medical Association*, March 24, 1975.

DeVries, H.A. "Exercise Intensity Threshold for Improvement of Cardiovascular-Respiratory Function in Older Men." *Geriatrics*, April 1971.

_____ . "Physiological Effects of an Exercise Training Regimen Upon Men Aged 52-88." *Journal of Gerontology* 25 (1970).

_____ . *Vigor Regained*. Englewood Cliffs, N.J.: Prentice-Hall, 1974.

_____ . "Prescription of Exercise for Older Men from Telemetered Exercise Heart Rate Data." Unpublished, undated paper.

DeVries, H.A., and Adams, G.M. "Comparison of Exercise Responses in Old and Young Men: 1. The Cardiac Effort/Total Body Effort Relationship." *Journal of Gerontology* 27 (1972).

_____ . "Electromyographic Comparison of Single Doses of Exercise and Meprobromate as to the Effects on Muscular Relaxation." *American Journal of Physical Medicine* 51 (1972).

Ducroquet, R.; Ducroquet, J.; and Ducroquet, P. *Walking and Limping*. Philadelphia: J.B. Lippincott, 1968.

Dutton, R.E. "The Executive and Physical Fitness." *Personnel Administration*, March/April 1966.

Ediger, D. "Charting Body Heat—in Color." *The Physician and Sportsmedicine*, January 1975.

Elrick, H., et al. "Indians Who Run 100 Miles on 15,000 Calories a Day." *The Physician and Sportsmedicine*, February 1976.

"Fitness Movement Seen Curbing High Cost of Illness to U.S. Industry." *Commerce Today*, February 3, 1975.

Fixx, J.F. *The Complete Book of Running*. New York: Random House, 1977.

Fletcher, C. *The New Complete Walker*. New York: Alfred A. Knopf, 1977.

Foss, M.L., et al. "Initial Work Tolerance of Extremely Obese Patients." *Archives of Physical Medicine and Rehabilitation*, February 1975.

Furlong, W.B. "The Fun in Fun." *Psychology Today*, June 1976.

Giguere, P. "Boston Marathon—Beating the Heat with

Common Sense and Water." *The Physician and Sportsmedicine*, June 1976.

Glasser, W. *Positive Addiction*. New York: Harper and Row, 1976.

Glover, B. and Shephard, J. *The Runner's Handbook*. NY: Viking Press, 1978.

Golding, L.A. "Effects of Physical Training Upon Total Serum Cholesterol Levels." *Research Quarterly*, December 1961.

Goldstein, J. "Walkers of the World, Unite!" *Fitness For Living*, May/June 1968.

Gwinup, G. "Effect of Exercise Alone on the Weight of Obese Women." *Archives of Internal Medicine*, May 1975.

Haberern, J. "The Fitness Finders Arrive." *Fitness For Living*, July/August 1970.

Hanrahan, P. "Smile and Drive Them Crazy." *Runner's World*, October 1976.

Harger, B.S., et al. "The Caloric Cost of Running." *Journal of the American Medical Association*, April 22, 1974.

Haskel, W., et al. "Plasma Lipids and Lipoproteins in Women Runners." Presented to American Heart Association, November 1975.

"Health Practices and Physical Health Status." *Physical Fitness Research Digest*, April 1976.

"Heat Peril In Distance Runs Spurs ACSM Guideline Alert." *The Physician and Sportsmedicine*, July 1975.

Hellerstein, H. "Exploring the Effects of Exercise on Hypertension." *The Physician and Sportsmedicine*, December 1976.

Henderson, J. *Long Slow Distance: The Humane Way To Train*. Mountain View, Calif.: World Publications, 1969.

_____ . "New Beginnings in Running." *Runner's World*, April 1976.

_____ . *Run Gently, Run Long*. Mountain View, Calif.: World Publications, 1974.

_____ . "The Six in Ten Who Break Down," *Runner's World*, Dec. 1975.

Higdon, H. *Fitness After Forty*. Mountain View, CA: World Publications 1977.

Hlavac, H.F. *The Foot Book*. Mountain View, CA: World Publications, 1977.

Hocking, J.H. "Do You Know How To Walk?" *Recreation*, May 1942.

"How To Get Fit? Just Put One Foot After Another." *Executive Fitness Newsletter*, February 25, 1978.

Howorth, M.D. "The Art and Technique of Walking." *Consumer Bulletin*, April 1973.

Illich, I., and Keen, S. "Medicine Is a Major Threat to Health." *Psychology Today*, May 1976.

Intercollege Research, eds. "Exercise: A Heartening Life-Lengthener?" *Intercollege Research*, Pennsylvania State University, January 1976.

Jackson, D.W., and Bailey, D. "Shin Splints in the Young Athlete: A Nonspecific Diagnosis." *The Physician and Sportsmedicine*, March 1975.

The Jogger, eds. "Harry Hlavac, Jogging Podiatrist." *The Jogger*, July/August 1976.

Kasch, F.W. "The Effects of Exercise on the Aging Process." *The Physician and Sportsmedicine*, June 1976.

————. "The Energy Cost of Walking and Hiking." *The Physician and Sportsmedicine*, July 1976.

————. "Physiological Variables During Ten Years of Endurance Exercise." *Medicine and Science in Sports* 8 (1976).

Kasch, F.W., et al. "Cardiovascular Changes in Middle-Aged Men During Two Years of Training." *Journal of Applied Physiology*, January 1973.

Katch, F.I., and McArdle, W.D. *Nutrition, Weight Control, and Exercise*. Boston, Mass.: Houghton, Mifflin, 1977.

Kavanaugh, T. "A Conditioning Programme for the Elderly." *Canadian Family Physician*, July 1971.

————. *Heart Attack? Counterattack!* Toronto: Van Nostrand Reinhold, 1976.

"Keeping Fit in the Company Gym." *Fortune*, October 1975.

Kiell, P.J. and Frelinghuysen, J.S. *Keep Your Heart Running.* New York: Winchester Press, 1976.

King, S. "United States Plans To Turn Old Rail Beds Into Recreation Trails." *The New York Times*, May 3, 1978.

Klaw, S. *The Great American Medical Show: The Unhealthy State of U.S. Medical Care and What Can Be Done About It.* NY: Viking Press, 1975.

Knowles, J. "Wiser Way of Living, Not Dramatic Cures Seen as Key to Health. Preventive Care to Become More Important." *Wall Street Journal*, 3/23/76.

Konecke, S.P. "Joggers' Foot and Leg Problems Can Be Helped." *The Jogger*, July/August 1976.

Kostrubala, T. *The Joy of Running.* Philadelphia: J.P. Lippincott, 1976.

Kuntzleman, C. *Activetics.* New York: Peter H. Wyden, 1975.

_____ . "Are Your Hormones Killing You?" *Fitness For Living*, November/December, 1970.

_____ . *Concepts In Health and Fitness.* Spring Arbor, Mich.: Arbor Press, 1978.

_____ . *The Exerciser's Handbook.* New York: David McKay, 1978.

_____ . *The Physical Fitness Encyclopedia.* Emmaus, Penn.: Rodale Books, 1970.

Kuntzleman, C.: and *Consumer Guide Magazine*, eds. *Rating The Exercises.* New York: William Morrow and Co., 1978.

Lake, A. "How Much Good Does Exercise Do You?" *Woman's Day*, October 1975.

Lance, K. *Running for Health and Beauty.* New York: Bobbs-Merrill, 1977.

Lawrence, R.M. "Race Walking for Everyone." *Today's Jogger*, March 1978.

Leonard, G. *The Ultimate Athlete.* New York: Viking Press, 1975.

_____ "The Holistic Health Revolution." *New West*, May 10, 1976.

Lewis, S., et al. "Effects of Physical Activity on Weight Reduction in Obese Middle Aged Women." *The American Journal of Clinical Nutrition* 29 (1976).

Lilliefors, J. "The Need to Fail." *Runner's World*, April 1976.

————— . "Training the Head." *Runner's World*, May 1976.

Loeschhorn, J. "Running Shoes." *WomenSports*, February 1976.

Lopez, S., et al. "Effect of Exercise and Physical Fitness on Serum Lipids and Lipoproteins." *Atherosclerosis* 20 (1974).

Luria, M.H., and Koepke, K.R. "The Physical Conditioning Effects of Walking." *Journal of Sports Medicine* 15 (1975).

McCormick. L. "Race Walker's Stride a Lonely Course In The United States." *Christian Science Monitor.* June 18, 1973.

McDermott, B. "Going Through Life at a Walk." *Sports Illustrated.* 5/8/78.

McGregor, M. "The Coronary Collateral Circulation." *Circulation*, October 1975.

McWhirter, N. *Guiness Book of World Records*, New York: Bantam Books, 1977.

"Man Called Prone to Extinction if Not Encouraged to Walk More." *Medical Tribune*, June 30, 1971.

Mahoney, M.J., and Mahoney, K. "Fight Fat with Behavior Control." *Psychology Today*, May 1976.

Mayes, D.S. "What's Round and Pounds the Ground? A Slogger!" *The Physician and Sportsmedicine*, April 1976.

"May Your Hearts Be Ever Young and Gay." *Executive Health* 10 (1973).

Menier, D.S., and Pugh, L.G.C.E. "The Relation of Oxygen Intake and Velocity of Walking and Running in Competition Walkers." *Journal of Physiology* 197 (1968).

Michener, J.A. *Sports in America*, New York: Random House, 1976.

Miller, B.F., and Galton, L. *Freedom from Heart Attacks.*

New York: Simon and Schuster, 1972.

Miller, G.J., and Miller N.E., "Plasma-High-Density-Lipoprotein Concentration and Development of Ischaemic Heart-Disease." *Lancet*, 1/4/75.

Milne, L.J., and Milne, M. *The Mountains*. New York: Time, 1962.

Mirkin, G. "A Key to Bad Knee Is a Fault in the Foot." *Washington Post*, June 17, 1976.

_____ . "Why Every Athlete Needs Muscle-Stretching Exercises." *Washington Post*, April 1, 1976.

_____ . "How Much Training Do You Need?" *Washington Post*, 6/3/76.

Mundth, E.D., and Austen, W.G. "Surgical Measures for Coronary Heart Disease." *New England Journal of Medicine*, July 3, 1975; July 10, 1975; and July 17, 1975.

Myers, C.R. "The Nationwide YMCA Cardiovascular Health Program." *Journal of Physical Education*, Summer 1976.

_____ . *The YMCA Physical Fitness Handbook*. New York: Popular Library, 1975.

Myers, C.R.; Golding, L.; and Sinning, W. eds. *The Y's Way to Physical Fitness*. Emmaus, Penn.: Rodale Press, 1973.

Napier, J. "The Antiquity of Human Walking." *Scientific American*, April 1967.

"National Adult Physical Fitness Survey." *The President's Council on Physical Fitness and Sports Newsletter*, May 1973.

National Geographic Society. *Wilderness U.S.A.* Washington, D.C.: National Geographic Society, 1973.

National Wildlife Federation. *Conservation Directory*. Washington, D.C.: The National Wildlife Federation, 1978.

Naughton, J., and Nagle, F. "Peak Oxygen Intake During Physical Fitness Program for Middle-Aged Men." *Journal of the American Medical Association*, March 15, 1965.

Nelson, C.M. "Rehabilitation Emphasis Should Be On

References / 125

Exercise." *The Physician and Sportsmedicine*, September 1976.

"New Rx For a Healthier Heart: 2,000 Calories of Sweat a Week." *Executive Fitness Newsletter*, January 14, 1978.

Norman, J. "The Tarahumaras: Mexico's Long Distance Runners." *National Geographic*, May 1976.

"On Walking...Nature's Own Amazing 'Anti-Age Antibiotic.' " *Executive Health* 14 (1978).

Overbeke, J.E. "Can Health Care Costs be Tamed?" *Industry Week*, 5/3/76.

Paffenberger, R.S., Jr.: and Hale, W.E. "Work Activity and Coronary Heart Mortality." *New England Journal of Medicine*, March 13, 1975.

Paul, L. "Sport Is a Three-Letter Word." *Intellectual Digest*. June 1974.

Pearson, K. "The Control of Walking." *Scientific American*, December 1976.

The Physician and Sportsmedicine, eds. "Achilles Tendon Problems Increase," *The Physician and Sportsmedicine*, March 1976.

_____ . "Balancing Heat Stress, Fluids, and Electrolytes." *The Physician and Sportsmedicine*, August, 1975.

_____ . "Exercise and the Heart." *The Physician and Sportsmedicine*, March 1974.

_____ . "Exercise Prescription Guidelines Listed." *The Physician and Sportsmedicine*, July 1975.

_____ . "Foot Problems in Runners." *The Physician and Sports Medicine*, July 1976.

_____ . "Overcoming Overprotection of the Elderly." *The Physician and Sportsmedicine*, June 1976.

_____ . "Roger Bannister: 'Human Beings Are Not The Same.' " *The Physician and Sportsmedicine*, September 1974.

_____ . "What to Cover in Office Evaluation for Exercise." *The Physician and Sportsmedicine*, June 1976.

"Pitcher Who Sets Two Records After MI Gets Heart Award." *Medical Tribune*, May 15, 1974.

Pollock, M.L. "How Much Exercise Is Enough?" *The Physician and Sportsmedicine*, June 1978.

Pollock, M.L., et al. "Effects of Walking on Body Composition and Cardiovascular Function of Middle Aged Men." *Journal of Applied Physiology*, January 1971.

_____ . "Physologic Responses of Men 49 to 65 Years of Age to Endurance Training." *American Geriatrics Society*, March 1976.

Pollock, M.L.; Wilmore, J.H.; and Fox, S.M. *Health and Fitness Through Physical Activity:* New York: John Wiley and Sons, 1978.

The President's Council on Physical Fitness and Sports. "Exercise and Weight Control" Washington, D.C.: Superintendent of Documents, United States Government Printing Office.

Pugh, L.G.C.E. "The Influence of Wind Resistance in Running and Walking and the Mechanical Efficiency of Work Against Horizontal or Vertical Forces." *Journal of Physiology* 213 (1971).

Rarick, G.L. *Physical Activity: Human Growth and Development.* New York: Academic Press, 1973.

Reed, R. "Going Walk-About in a Jumbo Jet." *Times of London*, July 17, 1976.

Renold, A.E., and Gahill, G.F. *Adipose Tissue.* Washington, D.C.: American Physiological Society, 1965.

Rinehart, L.M. "Exercise: The Key to a Healthy Old Age." *Fitness For Living*, July/August 1973.

Rodale, R. "Walk Before You Run." *Fitness For Living*, May/June 1969.

_____ . "Take a Long Walk!" *Fitness For Living*, March/April 1969.

Rose, C.L., and Cohen, M.L. "Relative Importance of Physical Activity for Longevity." Unpublished report of a study conducted at Veterans Administration Outpatient Clinic, Boston.

Rudner, R. *Off and Walking.* New York: Holt, Rinehart, and Winston, 1977.

Ruffer, W.A. "A Study of Extreme Physical Activity Groups of Young Men." *Research Quarterly*, May 1965.

Runner's World, eds. "The 1979 Runner's World Shoe Survey." *Runner's World*, October 1978.

Ryan, A.J. "Aging, Exercise, and Longevity." *The Physician and Sportsmedicine*, June 1975.

_____. "Carotid Palpation Practice Questioned." *The Physician and Sportsmedicine*, September 1976.

_____. "Heat Stress and the Vulnerable Athlete." *The Physician and Sportsmedicine*, June 1973.

Ryan, A.J.; and Allman F.L., Jr. *Sports Medicine*, New York: Academic Press, 1974.

Ryan, A.J.; Dempsey, J.A.; Gordon, E.S.; Foss, M.L.; and Oscai, L.D. "Charting the Factors of Fatness: A Round Table." *The Physician and Sportsmedicine*, July 1975.

Seder, J.I. "Heel Injuries Incurred in Running and Jumping." *The Physician and Sportsmedicine*, October 1976.

Selye, H. "Stress." *Intellectual Digest*, June 1974.

_____. *Stress Without Distress*. Philadelphia: J.P. Lippincott, Inc.

_____. The Stress of Life. New York : McGraw-Hill, 1956.

Sheehan, G. "Come and Play." *The Physician and Sportsmedicine*, Nov. 1974.

_____. "Let Me Do My Thing—And You Can Do Yours." *The Physician and Sportsmedicine*, June 1975.

_____. "Let's Hear It for Morton's Foot." *The Physician and Sportsmedicine*, March 1974.

_____. *Running and Being: "The Total Experience."* New York: Simon and Schuster, 1978.

Stamford, B.A.; Hambacher, W.; and Fallica, A. "Effects of Daily Physical Exercise on the Psychiatric State of Institutionalized Geriatric Mental Patients." *The Research Quarterly*, March 1974.

Stone, F. "Staying in Shape for the Rigors of Management '75: 1. A Sound Mind..." *Management Review*, January 1975.

Sussman, A., and Goode, R. *The Magic of Walking*. New York: Simon and Schuster, 1967.

"The Fitness Mania." *United States News and World Report*, 2/27/78.

Thomas C.T. "Help For Tired, Aching Legs." *Fitness For Living*, November/December 1971.

Thomson, P. "Fifty-Five Men, Women, and Grandfathers Have Hiked all 2,025 Miles of the Appalachian Trail." *The New York Times*, May 9, 1971.

Tosetti, J. "Tips on Dealing with Lightening on the Links." *The Physician and Sportsmedicine*, May 1976.

Turner, R., and Ball, K. "The Cardiologist's Responsibility for Preventing Coronary Heart Disease." *American Heart Journal*, February 1976.

Van Aaken, E. *The Van Aaken Method*, Mountain View, Calif: World Publications, 1976.

Van Dyck, D. "Big Brother Wants You To Take A Walk!" *Detroit Free Press*, July 12, 1978.

"Walk Away From Emphysema." *Fitness For Living*, Sept./October 1969.

Watts, M.T., "The Story of a Single Footpath." *Fitness For Living*, September/October 1968.

White, J.R., and Hung, H.F. "When Doctors Test Themselves, the Prescription is Exercise." *The Physician and Sportsmedicine*, December 1975.

"Will Exercise Improve Your Production?" *Pilot's Log*. New England Mutual Life Insurance Company, September 1976.

Wilmore, J. *Exercise And Science Reviews*. New York: Academic Press (assorted volumes).

Wilson, N.L., ed. *Obesity*. Philadelphia: F.A. Davis, 1969.

Wood, P.D. "Bos(huff)ton(puff)or(sigh) Bust." *The New York Times*, 4/21/75.

_____ . "Concentrations of Plasma Lipids and Lipoproteins in Male and Female Long-Distance Runners." Paper presented at International Congress of Physical Activity Sciences, Quebec, 1976.